OSHA 30-Hour
General Industry

Student Workbook

Raúl Ross Pineda
compiler

OSHA Outreach Training Program Series

OSHA 30-Hour General Industry; Student Workbook
OSHA Outreach Training Program Series
© Raúl Ross Pineda
Chicago, Illinois, USA
V.1 May 2018
ISBN-13: 978-1719167451
ISBN-10: 1719167451

OSHA 30-Hour General Industry
Student Workbook

This book contains handouts for the OSHA Outreach Training Program's 30-Hour General Industry course. It includes pamphlets that highlight the key points to be presented by the instructor, as well as the quizzes to be used as knowledge checks during class.

This book is a compilation of reading materials relevant to each class in the course, including the ones provided by OSHA specifically for the *Introduction to OSHA* class plus other materials provided in the *Publications* section at osha.gov. The quizzes were extracted from the PowerPoint presentations also provided by OSHA for this course, as reviewed on May, 2018.

Raúl Ross Pineda (mxsinfronteras@gmail.com) has worked for over 30 years in construction and general industry. He is an OSHA Authorized Trainer at the Latino Worker Safety Center (obrerolatino.org).

Content

Introduction to OSHA	1
Job safety and health it's the law. OSHA; 2015.	2
Employers must provide and pay for most PPE. OSHA.	3
Your rights as a whistleblower. Fact Sheet. OSHA; 2013.	4
We are OSHA, we can help. OSHA; 2015.	8
Activity: Ways to report workplace hazards. OSHA.	12
Workers rights practice worksheet; Crossword Puzzle. OSHA.	13
Introduction to Industrial Hygiene	15
Industrial Hygiene. OSHA.	16
Introduction to industrial hygiene. Knowledge check. OSHA.	24
Safety and Health Program	25
Introduction. Recommended Practices for Safety and Health Programs. OSHA; 2016	26
Safety and health program. Knowledge check. OSHA.	33
Personal protective equipment	35
Personal Protective Equipment. Fact Sheet. OSHA; 2006.	36
PPE for Workers Checklist.	38
Personal protective equipment. Knowledge check. OSHA.	39
Materials handling	41
Warehousing. Worker Safety Series. OSHA.	42
Materials handling. Knowledge check. OSIIA.	45
Hazard communication	47
Hazard Communication Safety Data Sheets. Quick Card. OSHA; 2016.	48
Hazard Communication Standard Labels. Quick Card. OSHA.	50
Hazard Communication Standard Pictogram. Quick Card. OSHA; 2016.	51
Hazard communication. Knowledge check. OSHA.	52
Hazardous materials	53
Steps to an Effective Hazard Communication Program for Employers That Use Hazardous Chemicals. Fact Sheet. OSHA; 2014.	54
Activity: Workplace Safety Analysis. OSHA.	57
Safety Data Sheet 32228. Restek.	64
Hazardous materials. Knowledge check. OSHA.	70
Walking and working surfaces, including fall protection	73
OSHA's Final Rule to Update, Align, and Provide Greater Flexibility in its General Industry Walking-Working Surfaces and Fall Protection Standards. Fact Sheet. OSHA; 2016.	74
Walking and working surfaces, including fall protection. Knowledge check. OSHA.	77

Fall protection — 79

Fall Protection in General Industry. Quick Card. OSHA. — 80

Slips, Trips and Falls. Fact Sheet. NCDOL. — 81

Fall protection. Knowledge check. OSHA. — 83

Electrical — 85

Electrical Safety. Quick Card. OSHA. — 86

Working Safely with Electricity. Fact Sheet. OSHA. — 87

Electrical. Knowledge check. OSHA. — 89

Machine guarding — 91

Amputations. Fact Sheet. OSHA; 2002. — 92

Machine guarding. Knowledge check. OSHA. — 94

Lockout and tagout — 97

Requirements of the standard. In Control of Hazardous Energy; Lockout/Tagout. OSHA; 2002. — 98

Permit-required confined spaces — 105

Introduction. In Permit-Required Confined Spaces. OSHA; 2004. — 106

Introduction to Ergonomics — 111

Factsheet A: What are musculoskeletal disorders? Preventing Sprains, Strains, and Repetitive Motion Injuries. State Building and Construction Trades Council of California, AFL-CIO; and Labor Occupational Health Program, University of California, Berkeley; 2012. — 112

Factsheet B: Risk factors for ergonomic injuries. Preventing Sprains, Strains, and Repetitive Motion Injuries. State Building and Construction Trades Council of California, AFL-CIO; and Labor Occupational Health Program, University of California, Berkeley; 2012. — 114

Introduction to Ergonomics. Knowledge check. OSHA. — 117

Bloodborne pathogens — 119

OSHA's Bloodborne Pathogens Standard. Fact Sheet. OSHA; 2011. — 120

Personal Protective Equipment (PPE) Reduces Exposure to Bloodborne Pathogens. Fact Sheet. OSHA; 2011. — 122

Bloodborne pathogens. Knowledge check. OSHA. — 124

Exit routes, Emergency Action Plans, Fire Prevention Plans, and fire protection — 127

Emergency Exit Routes. Fact Sheet. OSHA; 2003. — 128

Planning and Responding to Workplace Emergencies. Fact Sheet. OSHA; 2004. — 131

Exit routes, Emergency Action Plans, Fire Prevention Plans, and fire protection. Knowledge check. OSHA. — 133

Managing safety and health — 137

Hazard Identification and Assessment. In Recommended Practices for Safety and Health Programs. OSHA; 2016. — 138

Hazard prevention and control. In Recommended Practices for Safety and Health Programs. OSHA; 2016. — 143

Introduction to OSHA

Job Safety and Health
IT'S THE LAW!

All workers have the right to:

- A safe workplace.
- Raise a safety or health concern with your employer or OSHA, or report a work-related injury or illness, without being retaliated against.
- Receive information and training on job hazards, including all hazardous substances in your workplace.
- Request an OSHA inspection of your workplace if you believe there are unsafe or unhealthy conditions. OSHA will keep your name confidential. You have the right to have a representative contact OSHA on your behalf.
- Participate (or have your representative participate) in an OSHA inspection and speak in private to the inspector.
- File a complaint with OSHA within 30 days (by phone, online or by mail) if you have been retaliated against for using your rights.
- See any OSHA citations issued to your employer.
- Request copies of your medical records, tests that measure hazards in the workplace, and the workplace injury and illness log.

This poster is available free from OSHA.

Contact OSHA. We can help.

Employers must:

- Provide employees a workplace free from recognized hazards. It is illegal to retaliate against an employee for using any of their rights under the law, including raising a health and safety concern with you or with OSHA, or reporting a work-related injury or illness.
- Comply with all applicable OSHA standards.
- Report to OSHA all work-related fatalities within 8 hours, and all inpatient hospitalizations, amputations and losses of an eye within 24 hours.
- Provide required training to all workers in a language and vocabulary they can understand.
- Prominently display this poster in the workplace.
- Post OSHA citations at or near the place of the alleged violations.

FREE ASSISTANCE to identify and correct hazards is available to small and medium-sized employers, without citation or penalty, through OSHA-supported consultation programs in every state.

1-800-321-OSHA (6742) • TTY 1-877-889-5627 • www.osha.gov

HANDOUT #4
Employers Must Provide and Pay for Most PPE

Personal Protective Equipment (PPE)

The Occupational Safety and Health Administration (OSHA) requires that employers protect you from workplace hazards that can cause injury or illness. Controlling a hazard at its source is the best way to protect workers. However, when engineering, work practice and administrative controls are not feasible or do not provide sufficient protection, employers must provide personal protective equipment (PPE) to you and ensure its use.

PPE is equipment worn to minimize exposure to a variety of hazards. Examples include items such as gloves, foot and eye protection, protective hearing protection (earplugs, muffs), hard hats and respirators.

Employer Obligations	Workers should:
✓ Performing a "hazard assessment" of the workplace to identify and control physical and health hazards. ✓ Identifying and providing appropriate PPE for employees. ✓ Training employees in the use and care of the PPE. ✓ Maintaining PPE, including replacing worn or damaged PPE. ✓ Periodically reviewing, updating and evaluating the effectiveness of the PPE program.	✓ Properly wear PPE ✓ Attend training sessions on PPE ✓ Care for, clean and maintain PPE, an ✓ Inform a supervisor of the need to repair or replace PPE.

Employers Must Pay for Personal Protective Equipment (PPE)

On May 15, 2008, a new OSHA rule about employer payment for PPE went into effect. With few exceptions, OSHA now requires employers to pay for personal protective equipment used to comply with OSHA standards. The final rule does not create new requirements regarding what PPE employers must provide.

The standard makes clear that employers cannot require workers to provide their own PPE and the worker's use of PPE they already own must be completely voluntary. Even when a worker provides his or her own PPE, the employer must ensure that the equipment is adequate to protect the worker from hazards at the workplace.

Examples of PPE that Employers Must Pay for Include:

- Metatarsal foot protection
- Rubber boots with steel toes
- Non-prescription eye protection
- Prescription eyewear inserts/lenses for full face respirators
- Goggles and face shields
- Fire fighting PPE (helmet, gloves, boots, proximity suits, full gear)
- Hard hats
- Hearing protection
- Welding PPE

HANDOUT #4
Employers Must Provide and Pay for Most PPE

Payment Exceptions under the OSHA Rule

Employers are not required to pay for some PPE in certain circumstances:
- Non-specialty safety-toe protective footwear (including steel-toe shoes or boots) and non-specialty prescription safety eyewear provided that the employer permits such items to be worn off the job site. (OSHA based this decision on the fact that this type of equipment is very personal, is often used outside the workplace, and that it is taken by workers from jobsite to jobsite and employer to employer.)
- Everyday clothing, such as long-sleeve shirts, long pants, street shoes, and normal work boots.
- Ordinary clothing, skin creams, or other items, used solely for protection from weather, such as winter coats, jackets, gloves, parkas, rubber boots, hats, raincoats, ordinary sunglasses, and sunscreen
- Items such as hair nets and gloves worn by food workers for consumer safety.
- Lifting belts because their value in protecting the back is questionable.
- When the employee has lost or intentionally damaged the PPE and it must be replaced.

OSHA Standards that Apply

OSHA General Industry PPE Standards
- 1910.132: General requirements and payment
- 1910.133: Eye and face protection
- 1910.134: Respiratory protection
- 1910.135: Head protection
- 1910.136: Foot protection
- 1910.137: Electrical protective devices
- 1910.138: Hand protection

OSHA Construction PPE Standards
- 1926.28: Personal protective equipment
- 1926.95: Criteria for personal protective equipment
- 1926.96: Occupational foot protection
- 1926.100: Head protection
- 1926.101: Hearing protection
- 1926.102: Eye and face protection
- 1926.103: Respiratory protection

There are also PPE requirements in shipyards and marine terminals and many standards on specific hazards, such as 1910.1030: Bloodborne pathogens and 1910.146: Permit-required confined spaces.

OSHA standards are online at www.osha.gov.

Sources:
- *Employers Must Provide and Pay for PPE*, New Jersey Work Environment Council (WEC) Fact Sheet
- *OSHA Standards, 1910.132(h) and 1926.95(d)*
- *Employer Payment for Personal Protective Equipment Final Rule*, Federal Register: November 15, 2007 (Volume 72, Number 220)

OSHA® FactSheet

Your Rights as a Whistleblower

You may file a complaint with OSHA if your employer retaliates against you by taking unfavorable personnel action because you engaged in protected activity relating to workplace safety or health, asbestos in schools, cargo containers, airline, commercial motor carrier, consumer product, environmental, financial reform, food safety, health insurance reform, motor vehicle safety, nuclear, pipeline, public transportation agency, railroad, maritime, and securities laws.

Whistleblower Laws Enforced by OSHA

Each law requires that complaints be filed within a certain number of days after the alleged retaliation.

- *Asbestos Hazard Emergency Response Act* (90 days)
- *Clean Air Act* (30 days)
- *Comprehensive Environmental Response, Compensation and Liability Act* (30 days)
- *Consumer Financial Protection Act of 2010* (180 days)
- *Consumer Product Safety Improvement Act* (180 days)
- *Energy Reorganization Act* (180 days)
- *Federal Railroad Safety Act* (180 days)
- *Federal Water Pollution Control Act* (30 days)
- *International Safe Container Act* (60 days)
- *Moving Ahead for Progress in the 21st Century Act* (motor vehicle safety) (180 days)
- *National Transit Systems Security Act* (180 days)
- *Occupational Safety and Health Act* (30 days)
- *Pipeline Safety Improvement Act* (180 days)
- *Safe Drinking Water Act* (30 days)
- *Sarbanes-Oxley Act* (180 days)
- *Seaman's Protection Act* (180 days)
- *Section 402 of the FDA Food Safety Modernization Act* (180 days)
- *Section 1558 of the Affordable Care Act* (180 days)
- *Solid Waste Disposal Act* (30 days)
- *Surface Transportation Assistance Act* (180 days)
- *Toxic Substances Control Act* (30 days)
- *Wendell H. Ford Aviation Investment and Reform Act for the 21st Century* (90 days)

Unfavorable Personnel Actions

Your employer may be found to have retaliated against you if your protected activity was a contributing or motivating factor in its decision to take unfavorable personnel action against you. Such actions may include:

- Applying or issuing a policy which provides for an unfavorable personnel action due to activity protected by a whistleblower law enforced by OSHA
- Blacklisting
- Demoting
- Denying overtime or promotion
- Disciplining
- Denying benefits
- Failing to hire or rehire
- Firing or laying off
- Intimidation
- Making threats
- Reassignment to a less desirable position, including one adversely affecting prospects for promotion
- Reducing pay or hours
- Suspension

Filing a Complaint

If you believe that your employer retaliated against you because you exercised your legal rights as an employee, contact OSHA as soon as possible because you must file your complaint within the legal time limits.

An employee can file a complaint with OSHA by visiting or calling the local OSHA office or sending a written complaint to the closest OSHA regional or area office. Written complaints may be filed by facsimile, electronic communication, hand delivery during business hours, U.S. mail (confirmation services recommended), or other third-party commercial carrier. The date of the postmark, facsimile, electronic communication, telephone call, hand delivery, delivery to a third-party commercial carrier, or in-person filing at an OSHA office is considered the date filed. No particular form is required and complaints may be submitted in any language.

For OSHA area office contact information, please call 1-800-321-OSHA (6742) or visit www.osha.gov/html/RAmap.html.

Upon receipt of a complaint, OSHA will first review it to determine whether it is valid on its face. All complaints are investigated in accord with the statutory requirements.

With the exception of employees of the U.S. Postal Service, public sector employees (those employed as municipal, county, state, territorial or federal workers) are not covered by the *Occupational Safety and Health Act* (OSH Act). Non-federal public sector employees and, except in Connecticut, New York, New Jersey, the Virgin Islands, and Illinois, private sector employees are covered in states which operate their own occupational safety and health programs approved by Federal OSHA. For information on the 27 State Plan states, call 1-800-321-OSHA (6742), or visit www.osha.gov/dcsp/osp/index.html.

A federal employee who wishes to file a complaint alleging retaliation due to disclosure of a substantial and specific danger to public health or safety or involving occupational safety or health should contact the Office of Special Counsel (www.osc.gov) and OSHA's Office of Federal Agency Programs (www.osha.gov/dep/enforcement/dep_offices.html).

Coverage of public sector employees under the other statutes administered by OSHA varies by statute. If you are a public sector employee and you are unsure whether you are covered under a whistleblower protection statute, call 1-800-321-OSHA (6742) for assistance, or visit www.whistleblowers.gov.

How OSHA Determines Whether Retaliation Took Place

The investigation must reveal that:

- The employee engaged in protected activity;
- The employer knew about or suspected the protected activity;
- The employer took an adverse action; and
- The protected activity motivated or contributed to the adverse action.

If the evidence supports the employee's allegation and a settlement cannot be reached, OSHA will generally issue an order, which the employer may contest, requiring the employer to reinstate the employee, pay back wages, restore benefits, and other possible remedies to make the employee whole. Under some of the statutes the employer must comply with the reinstatement order immediately. In cases under the *Occupational Safety and Health Act*, *Asbestos Hazard Emergency Response Act*, and the *International Safe Container Act*, the Secretary of Labor will file suit in federal district court to obtain relief.

Partial List of Whistleblower Protections

Whistleblower Protections under the OSH Act

The OSH Act protects workers who complain to their employer, OSHA or other government agencies about unsafe or unhealthful working conditions in the workplace or environmental problems. You cannot be transferred, denied a raise, have your hours reduced, be fired, or punished in any other way because you used any right given to you under the OSH Act. Help is available from OSHA for whistleblowers.

If you have been punished or discriminated against for using your rights, you must file a complaint with OSHA within 30 days of the alleged reprisal for most complaints. No form is required, but you must send a letter or call the OSHA Area Office nearest you to report the discrimination (within 30 days of the alleged discrimination).

You have a limited right under the OSH Act to refuse to do a job because conditions are hazardous. You may do so under the OSH Act only when (1) you believe that you face death or serious injury (and the situation is so clearly hazardous that any reasonable person would believe the same thing); (2) you have tried, where possible, to get your employer to correct the condition, and been unable to obtain a correction and there is no other way to do the job safely; and (3) the situation is so urgent that you do not have time to eliminate the hazard through regulatory channels such as calling OSHA. For details, see www.osha.gov/as/opa/worker/refuse.html. OSHA cannot enforce union contracts or state laws that give employees the right to refuse to work.

Whistleblower Protections in the Transportation Industry

Employees whose jobs directly affect commercial motor vehicle safety or security are protected from retaliation by their employers for, among other things, reporting violations of federal or state commercial motor carrier safety or security regulations, or refusing to operate a vehicle because of violations of federal commercial motor vehicle safety or security regulations or because they have a reasonable apprehension of death or serious injury to themselves or the public and they have sought from the employer and been unable to obtain correction of the hazardous condition.

Similarly, employees of air carriers, their contractors or subcontractors who raise safety concerns or report violations of FAA rules and regulations are protected from retaliation, as are employees of owners and operators of pipelines, their contractors and subcontractors who report violations of pipeline safety rules and regulations. Employees involved in international shipping who report unsafe shipping containers are also protected. In addition, employees of railroad carriers or public transportation agencies, their contractors or subcontractors who report safety or security conditions or violations of federal rules and regulations relating to railroad or public transportation safety or security are protected from retaliation.

Whistleblower Protections for Voicing Environmental Concerns

A number of laws protect employees from retaliation because they report violations of environmental laws related to drinking water and water pollution, toxic substances, solid waste disposal, air quality and air pollution, asbestos in schools, and hazardous waste disposal sites. The *Energy Reorganization Act* protects employees from retaliation for raising safety concerns in the nuclear power industry and in nuclear medicine.

Whistleblower Protections When Reporting Corporate Fraud

Employees who work for publicly traded companies or companies required to file certain reports with the Securities and Exchange Commission are protected from retaliation for reporting alleged mail, wire, bank or securities fraud; violations of SEC rules or regulations of the SEC; or violations of federal laws relating to fraud against shareholders.

Whistleblower Protections for Voicing Consumer Product Concerns

Employees of consumer product manufacturers, importers, distributors, retailers, and private labelers are protected from retaliation for reporting reasonably perceived violations of any statute or regulation within the jurisdiction of the Consumer Product Safety Commission.

More Information

To obtain more information on whistleblower laws, go to www.whistleblowers.gov.

This is one of a series of informational fact sheets highlighting OSHA programs, policies, or standards. It does not impose any new compliance requirements. For a comprehensive list of compliance requirements of OSHA standards and regulations, refer to Title 29 of the Code of Federal Regulations. Because some of these whistleblower laws have only recently been enacted, the final regulations implementing them may not yet be available in the Code of Federal Regulations but the laws are still being enforced by OSHA. This information will be made available to sensory-impaired individuals upon request. Voice phone number: (202) 693-1999; teletypewriter (TTY) number: (877) 889-5627.

For assistance, contact us. We can help. It's confidential.

U.S. Department of Labor
www.osha.gov (800) 321-OSHA (6742)

DWP FS-3638 04/2013

We Are OSHA

We Can Help

Workers' rights under the OSH Act
Workers are entitled to working conditions that do not pose a risk of serious harm. To help assure a safe and healthful workplace, OSHA also provides workers with the right to:

- Ask OSHA to inspect their workplace;
- Use their rights under the law without retaliation;
- Receive information and training about hazards, methods to prevent harm, and the OSHA standards that apply to their workplace. The training must be in a language you can understand;
- Get copies of test results done to find hazards in the workplace;
- Review records of work-related injuries and illnesses; and
- Get copies of their medical records.

OSHA®
Occupational Safety and Health Administration
U.S. Department of Labor

Who OSHA covers

Private sector workers
Most employees in the nation come under OSHA's jurisdiction. OSHA covers private sector employers and employees in all 50 states, the District of Columbia, and other U.S. jurisdictions either directly through Federal OSHA or through an OSHA-approved state program. State-run health and safety programs must be at least as effective as the Federal OSHA program. To find the contact information for the OSHA Federal or State Program office nearest you, call 1-800-321-OSHA (6742) or go to www.osha.gov.

State and local government workers
Employees who work for state and local governments are not covered by Federal OSHA, but have OSH Act protections if they work in those states that have an OSHA-approved state program. The following 22 states or territories have OSHA-approved programs:

Alaska	Arizona	California
Hawaii	Indiana	Iowa
Kentucky	Maryland	Michigan
Minnesota	Nevada	New Mexico
North Carolina	Oregon	South Carolina
Tennessee	Utah	Vermont
Virginia	Washington	Wyoming
Puerto Rico		

Five additional states and one U.S. territory have OSHA-approved plans that cover public sector workers only:

Connecticut	Illinois	Maine
New Jersey	New York	Virgin Islands

Private sector workers in these five states and the Virgin Islands are covered by Federal OSHA.

Federal government workers

Federal agencies must have a safety and health program that meets the same standards as private employers. Although OSHA does not fine federal agencies, it does monitor federal agencies and responds to workers' complaints. The United States Postal Service (USPS) is covered by OSHA.

Not covered under the OSH Act:
- Self-employed;
- Immediate family members of farm employers who do not employ outside employees;
- Workplace hazards regulated by another federal agency (for example, the Mine Safety and Health Administration, the Department of Energy, or Coast Guard).

OSHA standards: Protection on the job

OSHA standards are rules that describe the methods that employers must use to protect their employees from hazards. There are OSHA standards for Construction work, Agriculture, Maritime operations, and General Industry, which are the standards that apply to most worksites. These standards limit the amount of hazardous chemicals workers can be exposed to, require the use of certain safe practices and equipment, and require employers to monitor hazards and keep records of workplace injuries and illnesses.

Examples of OSHA standards include requirements to provide fall protection, prevent trenching cave-ins, prevent some infectious diseases, assure that workers safely enter confined spaces, prevent exposure to harmful substances like asbestos, put guards on machines, provide respirators or other safety equipment, and provide training for certain dangerous jobs.

Employers must also comply with the General Duty Clause of the OSH Act, which *requires employers to keep their workplace free of serious recognized hazards*. This clause is generally cited when no OSHA standard applies to the hazard.

Workers can ask OSHA to inspect their workplace

Workers, or their representatives, may file a complaint and ask OSHA to inspect their workplace if they believe there is a serious hazard or that their employer is not following OSHA standards. A worker can tell OSHA not to let their employer know who filed the complaint. **It is a violation of the OSH Act for an employer to fire, demote, transfer or retaliate in any way against a worker for filing a complaint or using other OSHA rights.**

Written complaints that are signed by a worker or their representative and submitted to the closest OSHA office are more likely to result in an on-site OSHA inspection. You can call 1-800-321-OSHA (6742) to request a complaint form from your local OSHA office or visit www.osha.gov/pls/osha7/eComplaintForm.html to submit the form online. Completed forms can also be faxed or mailed to the local OSHA office. Most complaints sent in online may be resolved informally over the phone with your employer.

When the OSHA inspector arrives, workers and their representatives have the right to:

- Go along on the inspection;
- Talk privately with the OSHA inspector; and
- Take part in meetings with the inspector and the employer before and after the inspection is conducted.

Where there is no union or employee representative, the OSHA inspector must talk confidentially with a reasonable number of workers during the course of the investigation.

When an inspector finds violations of OSHA standards or serious hazards, OSHA may issue citations and fines. A citation includes the methods an employer may use to fix a problem and the date by when the corrective actions must be completed. Workers only have the right to challenge the deadline for when a problem must be resolved. Employers, on the other hand, have the right to contest whether there is a violation or any other part of the citation. Workers or their representatives must notify OSHA that they want to be involved in the appeals process if the employer challenges a citation.

If you send in a complaint requesting an OSHA inspection, you have the right to find out the results of the OSHA inspection and request a review if OSHA does not issue citations.

Employer responsibilities

Employers have the responsibility to provide a safe workplace. **Employers MUST provide their employees with a workplace that does not have serious hazards and must follow all OSHA safety and health standards.** Employers must find and correct safety and health problems. OSHA further requires employers to try to eliminate or reduce hazards first by making changes in working conditions rather than just relying on masks, gloves, earplugs or other types of personal protective equipment. Switching to safer chemicals, implementing processes to trap harmful fumes, or using ventilation systems to clean the air are examples of effective ways to get rid of or minimize risks.

Employers **MUST** also:

- Prominently display the official OSHA *Job Safety and Health – It's the Law* poster that describes rights and responsibilities under the OSH Act. **This poster is free and can be downloaded from www.osha.gov.**
- Inform workers about chemical hazards through training, labels, alarms, color-coded systems, chemical information sheets and other methods.
- Provide safety training to workers in a language and vocabulary they can understand.
- Keep accurate records of work-related injuries and illnesses.
- Perform tests in the workplace, such as air sampling, required by some OSHA standards.
- Provide required personal protective equipment at no cost to workers.*
- Provide hearing exams or other medical tests required by OSHA standards.

 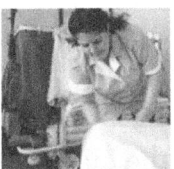 

- Post OSHA citations and injury and illness data where workers can see them.
- Notify OSHA within 8 hours of a workplace fatality or within 24 hours of any work-related inpatient hospitalization, amputation or loss of an eye (1-800-321-OSHA [6742]).
- Not retaliate against workers for using their rights under the law, including their right to report a work-related injury or illness.

* Employers must pay for most types of required personal protective equipment.

The law protects workers from retaliation when using their OSHA rights

The OSH Act protects workers who complain to their employer, OSHA or other government agencies about unsafe or unhealthful working conditions in the workplace or environmental problems. You cannot be transferred, denied a raise, have your hours reduced, be fired, or punished in any other way because you used any right given to you under the OSH Act. Help is available from OSHA for whistleblowers.

If you have been punished or retaliated against for using your rights, you must file a complaint with OSHA **within 30 days** from the date the retaliatory decision was both made and communicated to you. No form is needed, but you must call OSHA within 30 days of the alleged retaliation at 1-800-321-OSHA (6742) and ask to speak to the OSHA area office nearest you to report the retaliation.

You have the right to a safe workplace

The *Occupational Safety and Health Act of 1970* (OSH Act) was passed to prevent workers from being killed or seriously harmed at work. The law requires that employers provide their employees with working conditions that are free of known dangers. The Act created the Occupational Safety and Health Administration (OSHA), which sets and enforces protective workplace safety and health standards. OSHA also provides information, training and assistance to workers and employers. Workers may file a complaint to have OSHA inspect their workplace if they believe that their employer is not following OSHA standards or there are serious hazards.

Contact us if you have questions or want to file a complaint. We will keep your information confidential. We are here to help you. Call our toll-free number at 1-800-321-OSHA (6742) or go to www.osha.gov.

Occupational Safety and Health Administration U.S. Department of Labor

1-800-321-OSHA (6742)   TTY 1-877-889-5627
www.osha.gov

OSHA 3334-09R 2015

Activity: Ways to Report Workplace Hazards

Instructions

Based on the following scenario, discuss how you would follow the *Ways to Report Workplace Hazards* to determine what reporting approach would be best. Read the questions listed below that when answered, provide the information important to reporting workplace hazards. Is any additional information needed?

Scenario

You have worked at Ben Brothers Woodworking for 8 years as a janitor. Ben Brothers is located at 88 Wren Street, Anytown, USA, 40001. The company makes and refinishes office furniture. You usually work the second shift, but come in early sometimes. You and at least 3 of your co-workers have been getting headaches when you are working in the warehouse and the propane operated forklift is running. You have had headaches over the past two months, at least twice a week. The forklift operator told you that there are a lot of problems with the forklift and it needs to be replaced. You reported your headaches to your supervisor. She told you to go outside until you felt better and that there was nothing more she could do. You did some research and found out that exposure to propane in a confined, unventilated area can cause headaches, dizziness, difficulty breathing and unconsciousness. There is no monitoring of the air in the warehouse. There is no union at the facility. You decide to report the hazards.

Questions

- Has anyone been injured or made ill as a result of this problem?
- How many employees work at the site and how many are exposed to the hazard?
- How and when are workers exposed? On what shifts does the hazard exist?
- What work is performed in the unsafe or unhealthful area?
- What type of equipment is used? Is it in good condition?
- What materials and/or chemicals are used?
- Have employees been informed or trained regarding hazardous conditions?
- What process and/or operation is involved? What kinds of work are done nearby?
- How often and for how long do employees work at the task that leads to their exposure?
- How long (to your knowledge) has the condition existed?
- Have any attempts been made to correct the problem? Have there been any "near-miss" incidents?

Topic 4: Workers Rights Practice Worksheet
Crossword Puzzle

OSHA Provides Workers the Right to:

Across

4. Hazard _____ and medical records
6. Information about _____ and illnesses in your workplace
7. A safe and _____ workplace
8. Complain or request hazard _____ from employer
9. Participate in an OSHA _____

Down

1. Know about _____ conditions
2. Be free from _____ for exercising safety and health rights
3. _____ as provided in the OSHA standards
5. File a complaint with _____

Introduction to industrial hygiene

INDUSTRIAL HYGIENE

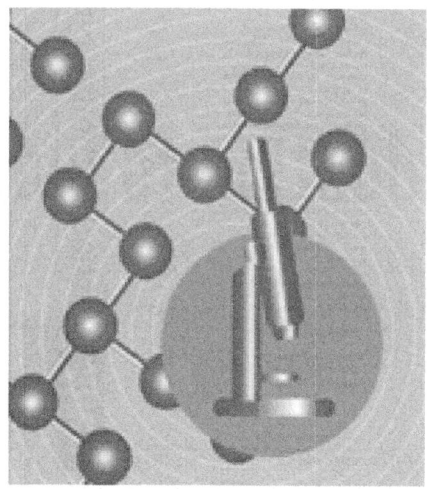

. . . *"that science and art devoted to the anticipation, recognition, evaluation, and control of those environmental factors or stresses arising in or from the workplace, which may cause sickness, impaired health and well-being, or significant discomfort among workers or among the citizens of the community."*

OSHA OFFICE OF TRAINING AND EDUCATION

These materials were developed by OSHA's Office of Training and Education and are intended to assist employers, workers, and others as they strive to improve workplace health and safety. While we attempt to thoroughly address specific topics, it is not possible to include discussion of everything necessary to ensure a healthy and safe working environment in a presentation of this nature. Thus, this information must be understood as a tool for addressing workplace hazards, rather than an exhaustive statement of an employer's legal obligations, which are defined by statute, regulations, and standards. Likewise, to the extent that this information references practices or procedures that may enhance health or safety, but which are not required by a statute, regulation, or standard, it cannot, and does not, create additional legal obligations. Finally, over time, OSHA may modify rules and interpretations in light of new technology, information, or circumstances; to keep apprised of such developments, or to review information on a wide range of occupational safety and health topics, you can visit OSHA's website at www.osha.gov.

INTRODUCTION

Industrial hygiene has been defined as "that science and art devoted to the anticipation, recognition, evaluation, and control of those environmental factors or stresses arising in or from the workplace, which may cause sickness, impaired health and well-being, or significant discomfort among workers or among the citizens of the community." Industrial hygienists use environmental monitoring and analytical methods to detect the extent of worker exposure and employ engineering, work practice controls, and other methods to control potential health hazards.

There has been an awareness of industrial hygiene since antiquity. The environment and its relation to worker health was recognized as early as the fourth century BC when Hippocrates noted lead toxicity in the mining industry. In the first century AD, Pliny the Elder, a Roman scholar, perceived health risks to those working with zinc and sulfur. He devised a face mask made from an animal bladder to protect workers from exposure to dust and lead fumes. In the second century AD, the Greek physician, Galen, accurately described the pathology of lead poisoning and also recognized the hazardous exposures of copper miners to acid mists.

In the Middle Ages, guilds worked at assisting sick workers and their families. In 1556, the German scholar, Agricola, advanced the science of industrial hygiene even further when, in his book *De Re Metallica*, he described the diseases of miners and prescribed preventive measures. The book included suggestions for mine ventilation and worker protection, discussed mining accidents, and described diseases associated with mining occupations such as silicosis.

Industrial hygiene gained further respectability in 1700 when Bernardo Ramazzini, known as the "father of industrial medicine," published in Italy the first comprehensive book on industrial medicine, *De Morbis Artificum Diatriba (The Diseases of Workmen)*. The book contained accurate descriptions of the occupational diseases of most of the workers of his time. Ramazzini greatly affected the future of industrial hygiene because he asserted that occupational diseases should be studied in the work environment rather than in hospital wards.

Industrial hygiene received another major boost in 1743 when Ulrich Ellenborg published a pamphlet on occupational diseases and injuries among gold miners. Ellenborg also wrote about the toxicity of carbon monoxide, mercury, lead, and nitric acid.

In England in the 18th century, Percival Pott, as a result of his findings on the insidious effects of soot on chimney sweepers, was a major force in getting the British Parliament to pass the *Chimney-Sweepers Act of 1788*. The passage of the English Factory Acts beginning in 1833 marked the first effective legislative acts in the field of industrial safety. The Acts, however, were intended to provide compensation for accidents rather than to control their causes. Later, various other European nations developed workers' compensation acts, which stimulated the adoption of increased factory safety precautions and the establishment of medical services within industrial plants.

In the early 20th century in the U.S., Dr. Alice Hamilton led efforts to improve industrial hygiene. She observed industrial conditions first hand and startled mine owners, factory managers, and state officials with evidence that there was a correlation between worker illness and exposure to toxins. She also presented definitive proposals for eliminating unhealthful working conditions.

At about the same time, U.S. federal and state agencies began investigating health conditions in industry. In 1908, public awareness of occupationally related diseases stimulated the passage of compensation acts for certain civil employees. States passed the first workers' compensation laws in 1911. And in 1913, the New York Department of Labor and the Ohio Department of Health established the first state industrial hygiene programs. All states enacted such legislation by 1948. In most states, there is some compensation coverage for workers contracting occupational diseases.

The U.S. Congress has passed three landmark pieces of legislation related to safeguarding workers' health: (1) the *Metal and Nonmetallic Mines Safety Act of 1966*, (2) the *Federal Coal Mine Safety and Health Act of 1969*, and (3) the *Occupational Safety and Health Act of 1970 (OSH Act)*. Today, nearly every employer is required to implement the elements of an industrial hygiene and safety, occupational health, or hazard communication program and to be responsive to the Occupational Safety and Health Administration (OSHA) and its regulations.

OSHA AND INDUSTRIAL HYGIENE

Under the *OSH Act*, OSHA develops and sets mandatory occupational safety and health requirements applicable to the more than 6 million workplaces in the U.S. OSHA relies on, among many others, industrial hygienists to evaluate jobs for potential health hazards. Developing and setting mandatory occupational safety and health standards involves determining the extent of employee exposure to hazards and deciding what is needed to control these hazards to protect workers. Industrial hygienists are trained to anticipate, recognize, evaluate, and recommend controls for environmental and physical hazards that can affect the health and well-being of workers.

More than 40 percent of the OSHA compliance officers who inspect America's workplaces are industrial hygienists. Industrial hygienists also play a major role in developing and issuing OSHA standards to protect workers from health hazards associated with toxic chemicals, biological hazards, and harmful physical agents. They also provide technical assistance and support to the agency's national and regional offices. OSHA also employs industrial hygienists who assist in setting up field enforcement procedures, and who issue technical interpretations of OSHA regulations and standards.

Industrial hygienists analyze, identify, and measure workplace hazards or stresses that can cause sickness, impaired health, or significant discomfort in workers through chemical, physical, ergonomic, or biological exposures. Two roles of the OSHA industrial hygienist are to spot those conditions and help eliminate or control them through appropriate measures.

WORKSITE ANALYSIS

A worksite analysis is an essential first step that helps an industrial hygienist determine what jobs and work stations are the sources of potential problems. During the worksite analysis, the industrial hygienist measures and identifies exposures, problem tasks, and risks. The most-effective worksite analyses include all jobs, operations, and work activities. The industrial hygienist inspects, researches, or analyzes how the particular chemicals or physical hazards at that worksite affect worker health. If a situation hazardous to health is discovered, the industrial hygienist recommends the appropriate corrective actions.

RECOGNIZING AND CONTROLLING HAZARDS

Industrial hygienists recognize that engineering, work practice, and administrative controls are the primary means of reducing employee exposure to occupational hazards.

Engineering controls minimize employee exposure by either reducing or removing the hazard at the source or isolating the worker from the hazard. Engineering controls include eliminating toxic chemicals and substituting non-toxic chemicals, enclosing work processes or confining work operations, and the installation of general and local ventilation systems.

Work practice controls alter the manner in which a task is performed. Some fundamental and easily implemented work practice controls include (1) changing existing work practices to follow proper procedures that minimize exposures while operating production and control equipment; (2) inspecting and maintaining process and control equipment on a regular basis; (3) implementing good housekeeping procedures; (4) providing good supervision; and (5) mandating that eating, drinking, smoking, chewing tobacco or gum, and applying cosmetics in regulated areas be prohibited.

Administrative controls include controlling employees' exposure by scheduling production and tasks, or both, in ways that minimize exposure levels. For example, the employer might schedule operations with the highest exposure potential during periods when the fewest employees are present.

When effective work practices or engineering controls are not feasible or while such controls are being instituted, appropriate **personal protective equipment** must be used. Examples of personal protective equipment are gloves, safety goggles, helmets, safety shoes, protective clothing, and respirators. To be effective, personal protective equipment must be individually selected, properly fitted and periodically refitted; conscientiously and properly worn; regularly maintained; and replaced, as necessary.

EXAMPLES OF JOB HAZARDS

To be effective in recognizing and evaluating on-the-job hazards and recommending controls, industrial hygienists must be familiar with the hazards' characteristics. Potential hazards can include air contaminants, and chemical, biological, physical, and ergonomic hazards.

Air Contaminants

These are commonly classified as either particulate or gas and vapor contaminants. The most common particulate contaminants include dusts, fumes, mists, aerosols, and fibers.

Dusts are solid particles generated by handling, crushing, grinding, colliding, exploding, and heating organic or inorganic materials such as rock, ore, metal, coal, wood, and grain

Fumes are formed when material from a volatilized solid condenses in cool air. In most cases, the solid particles resulting from the condensation react with air to form an oxide.

The term **mist** is applied to liquid suspended in the atmosphere. Mists are generated by liquids condensing from a vapor back to a liquid or by a liquid being dispersed by splashing or atomizing. **Aerosols** are also a form of a mist characterized by highly respirable, minute liquid particles.

Fibers are solid particles whose length is several times greater than their diameter, such as asbestos.

Gases are formless fluids that expand to occupy the space or enclosure in which they are confined. They are atomic, diatomic, or molecular in nature as opposed to droplets or particles which are made up of millions of atoms or molecules. Through evaporation, liquids change into vapors and mix with the surrounding atmosphere. **Vapors** are the volatile form of substances that are normally in a solid or liquid state at room temperature and pressure. Vapors are gases in that true vapors are atomic or molecular in nature.

Chemical Hazards

Harmful chemical compounds in the form of solids, liquids, gases, mists, dusts, fumes, and vapors exert toxic effects by inhalation (breathing), absorption (through direct contact with the skin), or ingestion (eating or drinking). Airborne chemical hazards exist as concentrations of mists, vapors, gases, fumes, or solids. Some are toxic through inhalation and some of them irritate the skin on contact; some can be toxic by absorption through the skin or through ingestion, and some are corrosive to living tissue.

The degree of worker risk from exposure to any given substance depends on the nature and potency of the toxic effects and the magnitude and duration of exposure. Information on the risk to workers from chemical hazards can be obtained from the Material Safety Data Sheet (MSDS) that OSHA's *Hazard Communication Standard* requires be supplied by the manufacturer or importer to the purchaser of all hazardous materials. The MSDS is a summary of the important health, safety, and toxicological information on the chemical or the mixture's ingredients. Other provisions of the Hazard Communication Standard require that all containers of hazardous substances in the workplace have appropriate warning and identification labels.

Biological Hazards

These include bacteria, viruses, fungi, and other living organisms that can cause acute and chronic infections by entering the body either directly or through breaks in the skin.

Occupations that deal with plants or animals or their products or with food and food processing may expose workers to biological hazards. Laboratory and medical personnel also can be exposed to biological hazards. Any occupations that result in contact with bodily fluids pose a risk to workers from biological hazards.

In occupations where animals are involved, biological hazards are dealt with by preventing and controlling diseases in the animal population as well as properly caring for and handling infected animals. Also, effective personal hygiene, particularly proper attention to minor cuts and scratches especially on the hands and forearms, helps keep worker risks to a minimum.

In occupations where there is potential exposure to biological hazards, workers should practice proper personal hygiene, particularly hand washing. Hospitals should provide proper ventilation, proper personal protective equipment such as gloves and respirators, adequate infectious waste disposal systems, and appropriate controls including isolation in instances of particularly contagious diseases such as tuberculosis.

Physical Hazards

These include excessive levels of ionizing and nonionizing electromagnetic radiation, noise, vibration, illumination, and temperature.

In occupations where there is exposure to ionizing radiation, **time**, **distance**, and **shielding** are important tools in ensuring worker safety. Danger from radiation increases with the amount of time one is exposed to it; hence, the shorter the time of exposure the smaller the radiation danger.

Distance also is a valuable tool in controlling exposure to both ionizing and nonionizing radiation. Radiation levels from some sources can be estimated by comparing the squares of the distances between the worker and the source. For example, at a reference point of 10 feet from a source, the radiation is 1/100 of the intensity at 1 foot from the source.

Shielding also is a way to protect against radiation. The greater the protective mass between a radioactive source and the worker, the lower the radiation exposure.

In some instances, however, limiting exposure to or increasing distance from certain forms of nonionizing radiation, such as lasers, is not effective. For example, an exposure to laser radiation that is faster than the blinking of an eye can be hazardous and would require workers to be miles from the laser source before being adequately protected. Shielding workers from this source can be an effective control method.

Noise, another significant physical hazard, can be controlled by various measures. Noise can be reduced by installing equipment and systems that have been engineered, designed, and built to operate quietly; by enclosing or shielding noisy equipment; by making certain that equipment is in good repair and properly maintained with all worn or unbalanced parts replaced; by mounting noisy equipment on special mounts to reduce vibration; and by installing silencers, mufflers, or baffles.

Substituting quiet work methods for noisy ones is another significant way to reduce noise-for example, welding parts rather than riveting them. Also, treating floors, ceilings, and walls with acoustical material can reduce reflected or reverberant noise. In addition, erecting sound barriers at adjacent work stations around noisy operations will reduce worker exposure to noise generated at adjacent work stations.

It is also possible to reduce noise exposure by increasing the distance between the source and the receiver, by isolating workers in acoustical booths, limiting workers' exposure time to noise, and by providing hearing protection. OSHA requires that workers in noisy surroundings be periodically tested as a precaution against hearing loss.

Another physical hazard, radiant heat exposure in factories such as steel mills, can be controlled by installing reflective shields and by providing protective clothing.

Ergonomic Hazards

The science of ergonomics studies and evaluates a full range of tasks including, but not limited to, lifting, holding, pushing, walking, and reaching. Many ergonomic problems result from technological changes such as increased assembly line speeds, adding specialized tasks, and increased repetition; some problems arise from poorly designed job tasks. Any of those conditions can cause ergonomic hazards such as excessive vibration and noise, eye strain, repetitive motion, and heavy lifting problems. Improperly designed tools or work areas also can be ergonomic hazards. Repetitive motions or repeated shocks over prolonged periods of time as in jobs involving sorting, assembling, and data entry can often cause irritation and inflammation of the tendon sheath of the hands and arms, a condition known as carpal tunnel syndrome.

Ergonomic hazards are avoided primarily by the effective design of a job or jobsite and by better designed tools or equipment that meet workers' needs in terms of physical environment and job tasks. Through thorough worksite analyses, employers can set up procedures to correct or control ergonomic hazards by using the appropriate engineering controls (e.g., designing or redesigning work stations, lighting, tools, and equipment); teaching correct work practices (e.g., proper lifting methods); employing proper administrative controls (e.g., shifting workers among several different tasks, reducing production demand, and increasing rest breaks); and, if necessary, providing and mandating personal protective equipment. Evaluating working conditions from an ergonomics standpoint involves looking at the total physiological and psychological demands of the job on the worker.
Overall, industrial hygienists point out that the benefits of a well-designed, ergonomic work environment can include increased efficiency, fewer accidents, lower operating costs, and more effective use of personnel.

In sum, industrial hygiene encompasses a broad spectrum of the working environment. Early in its history, OSHA recognized industrial hygiene as an integral part of a healthful work setting. OSHA places a high priority on using industrial hygiene concepts in its health standards and as a tool for effective enforcement of job safety and health regulations. By recognizing and applying the principles of industrial hygiene to the work environment, America's workplaces will become more healthful and safer.

Introduction to Industrial Hygiene

Knowledge check

1. Which of the following is an example of an industrial hygiene health hazard?

    a) Chemical hazards

    b) Economic hazards

    c) Electrical hazards

    d) Fall hazards

2. Which of the following is an example of a physical health hazard?

    a) Asbestos

    b) Noise

    c) Silica

    d) Lead

3. Which of the following controls is an example of an engineering control for protection against chemicals?

    a) Ventilation

    b) Respirators

    c) Training

    d) Signage

Safety and health program

INTRODUCTION

THESE RECOMMENDED PRACTICES provide responsible employers, workers, and worker representatives[3] with a sound, flexible framework for addressing safety and health issues in diverse workplaces. They may be used in any workplace, but will be particularly helpful in small and medium-sized workplaces. They can be applied equally well in traditional, fixed manufacturing workplaces and in the service sector, healthcare, retail, and even mobile or office-based work environments. They also include information specifically aimed at temporary worker and multiemployer work situations. Separate recommended practices are available for the construction industry.

---

3 Worker participation is vital to the success of the program. In several places in this document, OSHA refers not just to workers but also to their representatives, such as labor unions or religious or community groups.

The recommended practices emphasize a proactive approach to managing workplace safety and health. Traditional approaches are often reactive—that is, actions are taken only *after* a worker is injured or becomes sick, a new standard or regulation is published, or an outside inspection finds a problem that must be corrected. Finding and fixing hazards *before* they cause injury or illness is a far more effective approach. Doing so avoids the direct and indirect costs of worker injuries and illnesses, and promotes a positive work environment.

The concept of continuous improvement is central to the recommended practices. As with any journey, the first step is often the most challenging. The idea is to begin with a basic program and grow from there. By initially focusing on achieving modest goals, monitoring performance, and evaluating outcomes, you can help your workplace progress, over time, along the path to higher levels of safety and health.

THE BENEFITS OF IMPLEMENTING THESE RECOMMENDED PRACTICES

Responsible employers know that the main goal of a safety and health program is to prevent workplace injuries, illnesses, and deaths, as well as the suffering and financial hardship these events can cause for workers, their families, and their employers.

Employers may find that implementing these recommended practices brings other benefits as well. The renewed or enhanced commitment to safety and health and the cooperative atmosphere between employers and workers have been linked to:

- Improvements in product, process, and service quality.
- Better workplace morale.
- Improved employee recruiting and retention.
- A more favorable image and reputation (among customers, suppliers, and the community).

A study of small employers in Ohio found that workers' compensation claims fell dramatically after working with OSHA's SHARP program to adopt programs similar to those described in these recommended practices.

average number of claims DECREASED **52%**

cost per claim DECREASED **80%**

average lost time per claim DECREASED **87%**

claims (per million dollars of payroll) DECREASED **88%**

Source: Ohio Bureau of Workers' Compensation (2011), Ohio 21(d) SHARP Program Performance Assessment.

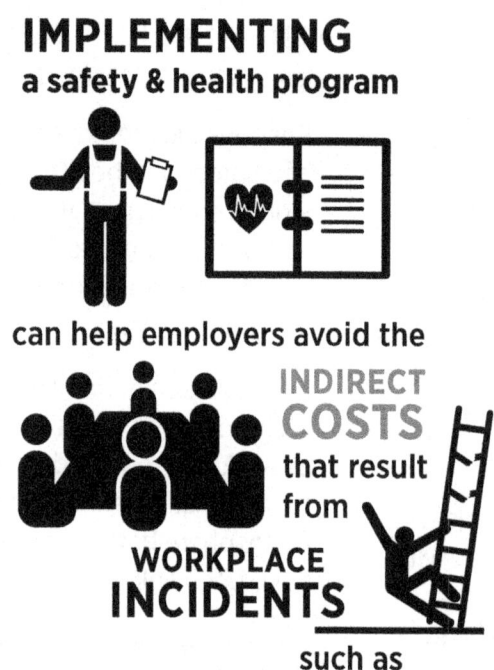

IMPLEMENTING a safety & health program can help employers avoid the **INDIRECT COSTS** that result from **WORKPLACE INCIDENTS** such as

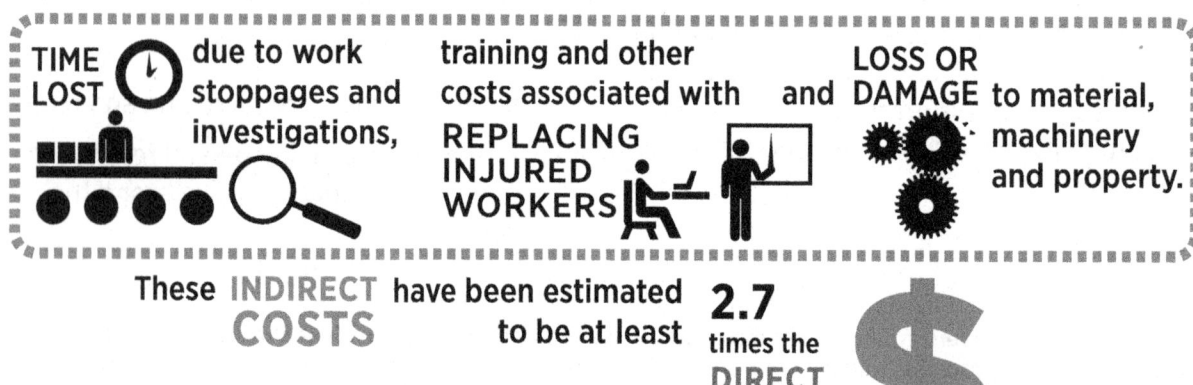

TIME LOST due to work stoppages and investigations, training and other costs associated with REPLACING INJURED WORKERS and LOSS OR DAMAGE to material, machinery and property.

These **INDIRECT COSTS** have been estimated to be at least **2.7** times the **DIRECT COSTS** $

Source: Leigh, J.P. (2011), Economic Burden of Occupational Injury and Illness in the United States. Milbank Quarterly, 89:728-772.[4]

HOW TO USE THE RECOMMENDED PRACTICES

Each section of the recommended practices describes a core program element (see page 7), followed by several action items. Each action item is an example of steps that employers and workers can take to establish, implement, maintain, and improve your safety and health program. You can use the self-evaluation tool found on the recommended practices Web page to track your progress and assess how fully you have implemented (or will implement) each action item.

Seven interrelated elements

The seven core elements are interrelated and are best viewed as part of an integrated system. Actions taken under one core element can (and likely will) affect actions needed under one or more other elements. For example, workers must be trained in reporting procedures and hazard identification techniques in order to be effective

---

[4] The 2.7 multiplier for indirect costs includes some social costs, such as workers' compensation costs not covered by insurance.

10 EASY THINGS TO GET YOUR PROGRAM STARTED

If these recommended practices appear challenging, here are some simple steps you can take to get started. Completing these steps will give you a solid base from which to take on some of the more structured actions presented in the recommended practices.

1. **SET SAFETY AND HEALTH AS A TOP PRIORITY**

   Always set safety and health as the top priority. Tell your workers that making sure they finish the day and go home safely is the way you do business. Assure them that you will work with them to find and fix any hazards that could injure them or make them sick.

2. **LEAD BY EXAMPLE**

   Practice safe behaviors yourself and make safety part of your daily conversations with workers.

3. **IMPLEMENT A REPORTING SYSTEM**

   Develop and communicate a simple procedure for workers to report any injuries, illnesses, incidents (including near misses/close calls), hazards, or safety and health concerns without fear of retaliation. Include an option for reporting hazards or concerns anonymously.

4. **PROVIDE TRAINING**

   Train workers on how to identify and control hazards using, for example, OSHA's Hazard Identification Training Tool.

5. **CONDUCT INSPECTIONS**

   Inspect the workplace with workers and ask them to identify any activity, piece of equipment, or material that concerns them. Use checklists, such as those included in OSHA's Small Business Handbook, to help identify problems.

6. **COLLECT HAZARD CONTROL IDEAS**

   Ask workers for ideas on improvements and follow up on their suggestions. Provide them time during work hours, if necessary, to research solutions.

7. **IMPLEMENT HAZARD CONTROLS**

   Assign workers the task of choosing, implementing, and evaluating the solutions they come up with.

8. **ADDRESS EMERGENCIES**

   Identify foreseeable emergency scenarios and develop instructions on what to do in each case. Meet to discuss these procedures and post them in a visible location in the workplace.

9. **SEEK INPUT ON WORKPLACE CHANGES**

   Before making significant changes to the workplace, work organization, equipment, or materials, consult with workers to identify potential safety or health issues.

10. **MAKE IMPROVEMENTS**

    Set aside a regular time to discuss safety and health issues, with the goal of identifying ways to improve the program.

participants. Thus, the "Education and Training" core element supports the "Worker Participation" core element. Similarly, setting goals (as described under "Management Leadership") will be more effective if you routinely evaluate your progress in meeting those goals (see "Program Evaluation and Improvement"). Progress in each core element is important to achieve maximum benefit from the program.

One size does not fit all

While the action items under each core element are specific, they are not prescriptive. The process described in these recommended practices can, and should, be tailored to the needs of each workplace. Likewise, your safety and health program can and should evolve. Experimentation, evaluation, and program modification are all part of the process. You may also experience setbacks from time to time. What is important is that you learn from setbacks, remain committed to finding out what works best for you, and continue to try different approaches.

Injuries and illnesses occur in all types of workplace settings, from manufacturing sites, to hospitals and healthcare facilities, to offices and service industries.[5] Workers can even be injured or become ill outside physical facilities, such as when driving a vehicle as part of a sales or service job. The preventive approaches described in these recommended practices work equally well across all sectors of the economy; for all different kinds of hazards; in both mobile and fixed work environments; and for small, medium-sized, and large organizations. Small employers may find that they can best accomplish the actions outlined in these recommended practices using informal communications and procedures. Larger employers, who have more complex work processes and hazards, may require a more formal and detailed program. They may also wish to integrate their safety and health program with other programs that they are using to manage production, quality control, and environmental protection or sustainability.

The importance of worker participation

Throughout these recommended practices, OSHA emphasizes the importance of worker participation in the safety and health program. For a program to succeed, workers (and, if applicable, their representatives) must participate in developing and implementing every element of the safety and health program. This emphasis on worker participation is consistent with the OSH Act, OSHA standards, and OSHA enforcement policies and procedures, which recognize the rights and roles of workers and their representatives in matters of workplace safety and health. Several action items described in these recommended practices rely on perspectives, expertise, and input that can come only from workers and their representatives.

When more than one employer is involved

Host employers, contractors, staffing agencies, and their workers should pay particular attention to the "Communication and Coordination for Host Employers, Contractors, and Staffing Agencies" section. This section describes actions that host employers and contractors, subcontractors, and temporary staffing agencies (and their workers) should take to ensure protection of everyone on the worksite.

For tools and resources to help you implement these recommended practices, visit: **www.osha.gov/shpguidelines**

---

5   Please note: OSHA has developed a separate document of *Recommended Practices for Safety and Health Programs for the Construction Industry*.

CORE ELEMENTS OF THE SAFETY AND HEALTH PROGRAM RECOMMENDED PRACTICES

MANAGEMENT LEADERSHIP	• Top management demonstrates its commitment to continuous improvement in safety and health, communicates that commitment to workers, and sets program expectations and responsibilities. • Managers at all levels make safety and health a core organizational value, establish safety and health goals and objectives, provide adequate resources and support for the program, and set a good example.
WORKER PARTICIPATION	• Workers and their representatives are involved in all aspects of the program—including setting goals, identifying and reporting hazards, investigating incidents, and tracking progress. • All workers, including contractors and temporary workers, understand their roles and responsibilities under the program and what they need to do to effectively carry them out. • Workers are encouraged and have means to communicate openly with management and to report safety and health concerns without fear of retaliation. • Any potential barriers or obstacles to worker participation in the program (for example, language, lack of information, or disincentives) are removed or addressed.
HAZARD IDENTIFICATION & ASSESSMENT	• Procedures are put in place to continually identify workplace hazards and evaluate risks. • Safety and health hazards from routine, nonroutine, and emergency situations are identified and assessed. • An initial assessment of existing hazards, exposures, and control measures is followed by periodic inspections and reassessments, to identify new hazards. • Any incidents are investigated with the goal of identifying the root causes. • Identified hazards are prioritized for control.
HAZARD PREVENTION & CONTROL	• Employers and workers cooperate to identify and select methods for eliminating, preventing, or controlling workplace hazards. • Controls are selected according to a hierarchy that uses engineering solutions first, followed by safe work practices, administrative controls, and finally personal protective equipment (PPE). • A plan is developed to ensure that controls are implemented, interim protection is provided, progress is tracked, and the effectiveness of controls is verified.
EDUCATION & TRAINING	• All workers are trained to understand how the program works and how to carry out the responsibilities assigned to them under the program. • Employers, managers, and supervisors receive training on safety concepts and their responsibility for protecting workers' rights and responding to workers' reports and concerns. • All workers are trained to recognize workplace hazards and to understand the control measures that have been implemented.
PROGRAM EVALUATION & IMPROVEMENT	• Control measures are periodically evaluated for effectiveness. • Processes are established to monitor program performance, verify program implementation, and identify program shortcomings and opportunities for improvement. • Necessary actions are taken to improve the program and overall safety and health performance.
COMMUNICATION AND COORDINATION FOR HOST EMPLOYERS, CONTRACTORS, AND STAFFING AGENCIES	• Host employers, contractors, and staffing agencies commit to providing the same level of safety and health protection to all employees. • Host employers, contractors, and staffing agencies commmunicate the hazards present at the worksite and the hazards that work of contract workers may create on site. • Host employers establish specifications and qualifications for contractors and staffing agencies. • Before beginning work, host employers, contractors, and staffing agencies coordinate on work planning and scheduling to identify and resolve any conflicts that could affect safety or health.

FOR MORE INFORMATION

For more information about these recommended practices, tools to help you implement them, and related topics, see the recommended practices Web page. This page includes links to many tools and resources developed by OSHA and others that can help employers and workers implement these recommended practices. OSHA will continue to update and add to this resource list.

OSHA's On-site Consultation Program offers free and confidential occupational safety and health services to small and medium-sized businesses in all states and several territories across the country, with priority given to high-hazard worksites.

On-site Consultation Program services are separate from enforcement and do not result in penalties or citations. Consultants from state agencies or universities work with employers to identify workplace hazards, provide advice on compliance with OSHA standards, and help them establish and improve their safety and health programs.

For free assistance, including help implementing your program, visit:
www.osha.gov/dcsp/smallbusiness
or call 1-800-321-6742 (OSHA)

Safety and health program

Knowledge check

1. Which of the following is a benefit from implementing an effective safety and health program?

    a) Higher morale of the workforce

    b) Improved company reputation

    c) Lower Worker Compensation Insurance rates

    d) All of the above

2. Which of the following is a direct cost of an accident?

    a) Lost production

    b) Retraining of new workers

    c) Physicians examination

    d) Poor customer relations

3. Employers must correct all identified hazards; however, which of the following hazards should the employer work to correct first?

    a) Guard missing on a piece of equipment, used every 6 months

    b) Broken rung on ladder, used daily by the entire crew

    c) Loose handrail on a dozer, used by a single equipment operator

    d) Wet floor by an eyewash station, in a path not travelled by personnel

Personal protective equipment

OSHA® FactSheet

Personal Protective Equipment

Personal protective equipment, or PPE, is designed to protect workers from serious workplace injuries or illnesses resulting from contact with chemical, radiological, physical, electrical, mechanical, or other workplace hazards. Besides face shields, safety glasses, hard hats, and safety shoes, protective equipment includes a variety of devices and garments such as goggles, coveralls, gloves, vests, earplugs, and respirators.

Employer Responsibilities

OSHA's primary personal protective equipment standards are in Title 29 of the Code of Federal Regulations (CFR), Part 1910 Subpart I, and equivalent regulations in states with OSHA-approved state plans, but you can find protective equipment requirements elsewhere in the General Industry Standards. For example, 29 CFR 1910.156, OSHA's Fire Brigades Standard, has requirements for firefighting gear. In addition, 29 CFR 1926.95-106 covers the construction industry. OSHA's general personal protective equipment requirements mandate that employers conduct a hazard assessment of their workplaces to determine what hazards are present that require the use of protective equipment, provide workers with appropriate protective equipment, and require them to use and maintain it in sanitary and reliable condition.

Using personal protective equipment is often essential, but it is generally the last line of defense after engineering controls, work practices, and administrative controls. Engineering controls involve physically changing a machine or work environment. Administrative controls involve changing how or when workers do their jobs, such as scheduling work and rotating workers to reduce exposures. Work practices involve training workers how to perform tasks in ways that reduce their exposure to workplace hazards.

As an employer, you must assess your workplace to determine if hazards are present that require the use of personal protective equipment. If such hazards are present, you must select protective equipment and require workers to use it, communicate your protective equipment selection decisions to your workers, and select personal protective equipment that properly fits your workers.

You must also train workers who are required to wear personal protective equipment on how to do the following:
- Use protective equipment properly,
- Be aware of when personal protective equipment is necessary,
- Know what kind of protective equipment is necessary,
- Understand the limitations of personal protective equipment in protecting workers from injury,
- Put on, adjust, wear, and take off personal protective equipment, and
- Maintain protective equipment properly.

Protection from Head Injuries

Hard hats can protect your workers from head impact, penetration injuries, and electrical injuries such as those caused by falling or flying objects, fixed objects, or contact with electrical conductors. Also, OSHA regulations require employers to ensure that workers cover and protect long hair to prevent it from getting caught in machine parts such as belts and chains.

Protection from Foot and Leg Injuries

In addition to foot guards and safety shoes, leggings (e.g., leather, aluminized rayon, or otherappropriate material) can help prevent injuries by protecting workers from hazards such as falling or rolling objects, sharp objects, wet and slippery surfaces, molten metals, hot surfaces, and electrical hazards.

Protection from Eye and Face Injuries

Besides spectacles and goggles, personal protective equipment such as special helmets or shields, spectacles with side shields, and faceshields can protect workers from the hazards of flying fragments, large chips, hot sparks, optical radiation, splashes from molten metals, as well as objects, particles, sand, dirt, mists, dusts, and glare.

Protection from Hearing Loss

Wearing earplugs or earmuffs can help prevent damage to hearing. Exposure to high noise levels can cause irreversible hearing loss or impairment as well as physical and psychological stress. Earplugs made from foam, waxed cotton, or fiberglass wool are self-forming and usually fit well. A professional should fit your workers individually for molded or preformed earplugs. Clean earplugs regularly, and replace those you cannot clean.

Protection from Hand Injuries

Workers exposed to harmful substances through skin absorption, severe cuts or lacerations, severe abrasions, chemical burns, thermal burns, and harmful temperatureextremes will benefit from hand protection.

Protection from Body Injury

In some cases workers must shield most or all of their bodies against hazards in the workplace, such as exposure to heat and radiation as well as hot metals, scalding liquids, body fluids, hazardous materials or waste, and other hazards. In addition to fire-retardant wool and fireretardant cotton, materials used in whole-body personal protective equipment include rubber, leather, synthetics, and plastic.

When to Wear Respiratory Protection

When engineering controls are not feasible, workers must use appropriate respirators to protect against adverse health effects caused by breathing air contaminated with harmful dusts, fogs, fumes, mists, gases, smokes, sprays, or vapors. Respirators generally cover the nose and mouth or the entire face or head and help prevent illness and injury. A proper fit is essential, however, for respirators to be effective. Required respirators must be NIOSH-approved and medical evaluation and training must be provided before use.

Additional Information

For additional information concerning protective equipment view the publication, Assessing the Need for Personal Protective Equipment: A Guide for Small Business Employers (OSHA 3151) available on OSHA's web site at www.osha.gov. For more information about personal protective equipment in the construction industry, visit www.osha-slc.gov/SLTC/constructionppe/index.html.

Contacting OSHA

To report an emergency, file a complaint or seek OSHA advice, assistance or products, call (800) 321-OSHA or contact your nearest OSHA regional or area office.

This is one in a series of informational fact sheets highlighting OSHA programs, policies or standards. It does not impose any new compliance requirements. For a comprehensive list of compliance requirements of OSHA standards or regulations, refer to Title 29 of the Code of Federal Regulations. This information will be made available to sensory impaired individuals upon request. The voice phone is (202) 693-1999; teletypewriter (TTY) number: (877) 889-5627.

For more complete information:

OSHA® Occupational Safety and Health Administration

U.S. Department of Labor
www.osha.gov
(800) 321-OSHA

DOC 4/2006

PPE for Workers Checklist

Protection	TYPICAL OPERATIONS OF CONCERN	YES	NO
EYE	Sawing, cutting, drilling, sanding, grinding, hammering, chopping, abrasive blasting, punch press operations, etc.		
	Pouring, mixing, painting, cleaning, siphoning, dip tank operations, dental and health care services, etc.		
	Battery charging, installing fiberglass insulation, compressed air or gas operations, etc.		
	Welding, cutting, laser operations, etc.		
FACE	Pouring, mixing, painting, cleaning, siphoning, dip tank operations, etc.		
	Welding, pouring molten metal, smithing, baking, cooking, drying, etc.		
	Cutting, sanding, grinding, hammering, chopping, pouring, mixing, painting, cleaning, siphoning, etc.		
HEAD	Work stations or traffic routes located under catwalks or conveyor belts, construction, trenching, utility work, etc.		
	Construction, confined space operations, building maintenance, etc.		
	Building maintenance; utility work; construction; wiring; work on or near communications, computer, or other high tech equipment; arc or resistance welding; etc.		
FEET	Construction, plumbing, smithing, building maintenance, trenching, utility work, grass cutting, etc.		
	Building maintenance; utility work; construction; wiring; work on or near communications, computer, or other high tech equipment; arc or resistance welding; etc.		
	Welding, foundry work, casting, smithing, etc.		
	Demolition, explosives manufacturing, grain milling, spray painting, abrasive blasting, work with highly flammable materials, etc.		
HANDS	Grinding, sanding, sawing, hammering, material handling, etc.		
	Pouring, mixing, painting, cleaning, siphoning, dip tank operations, health care and dental services, etc.		
	Welding, pouring molten metal, smithing, baking, cooking, drying, etc.		
	Building maintenance; utility work; construction; wiring; work on or near communications, computer, or other high tech equipment; arc or resistance welding; etc.		
BODY	Pouring, mixing, painting, cleaning, siphoning, dip tank operations, machining, sawing, battery charging, installing fiberglass insulation, compressed air or gas operations, etc.		
	Cutting, grinding, sanding, sawing, glazing, material handling, etc.		
	Welding, pouring molten metal, smithing, baking, cooking, drying, etc.		
	Pouring, mixing, painting, cleaning, siphoning, dip tank operations, etc.		
HEARING	Machining, grinding, sanding, work near conveyors, pneumatic equipment, generators, ventilation fans, motors, punch and brake presses, etc. Samples shown are: ear muffs (left) and earplugs (right)		

NOTE: Pictures of PPE are intended to provide a small sample of what the protection gear may look like. They are not to scale nor are they inclusive of all protection gear required and/or that is available.

Personal protective equipment

Knowledge check

1. Common causes of foot injuries include: crushing, penetration, molten metal, chemicals, slippery surfaces, and sharp objects.

    a) True

    b) False

2. Who is responsible for providing PPE needed to comply with OSHA standards?

    a) The employee

    b) OSHA

    c) The employer

    d) Workers' Compensation

3. Hazard controls must be addressed in which order of priority?

    a) Substitution, PPE, workaround, and administrative

    b) Workaround, stop work, PPE, and engineering

    c) Stop work, PPE, engineering, and substitution

    d) Substitution, engineering, administrative, and PPE

4. Which type of hard hat would provide the most protection from electrical hazards?

    a) Class A

    b) Class C

    c) Class E

    d) Class G

5. Hearing protection is required when noise levels exceed OSHA's PEL of ___ dBA as a TWA.
    a) 80
    b) 90
    c) 100
    d) 110

6. Who is responsible for providing specialized work footwear?
    a) Insurance companies
    b) The employee
    c) OSHA
    d) The employer

7. Which of the following is considered approved eye protection?
    a) Sun glasses
    b) Prescription glasses
    c) Reading glasses
    d) Glasses meeting ANSI standard Z87

8. Which of the following is NOT considered PPE?
    a) Rubber gloves
    b) Glasses meeting ANSI standard Z87
    c) Sports shoes
    d) Hearing muffs

Materials handling

UNITED STATES DEPARTMENT OF LABOR

Worker Safety Series
Warehousing

Think Safety

- More than 145,000 people work in over 7,000 warehouses.
- The fatal injury rate for the warehousing industry is higher than the national average for all industries.
- Potential hazards for workers in warehousing:
  - Unsafe use of forklifts;
  - Improper stacking of products;
  - Failure to use proper personal protective equipment;
  - Failure to follow proper lockout/tagout procedures;
  - Inadequate fire safety provisions; or
  - Repetitive motion injuries.

Think Safety Checklists

The following checklists may help you take steps to avoid hazards that cause injuries, illnesses and fatalities. As always, be cautious and seek help if you are concerned about a potential hazard.

General Safety

- Exposed or open loading dock doors and other areas that employees could fall 4 feet or more or walk off should be chained off, roped off or otherwise blocked.
- Floors and aisles are clear of clutter, electrical cords, hoses, spills and other hazards that could cause employees to slip, trip or fall.
- Proper work practices are factored into determining the time requirements for an employee to perform a task.
- Employees performing physical work have adequate periodic rest breaks to avoid fatigue levels that could result in greater risk of accidents and reduced quality of work.
- Newly-hired employees receive general ergonomics training and task-specific training.
- The warehouse is well ventilated.
- Employees are instructed on how to avoid heat stress in hot, humid environments.
- Employees are instructed on how to work in cold environments.
- The facility has lockout/tagout procedures.

Materials Handling Safety

- There are appropriately marked and sufficiently safe clearances for aisles and at loading docks or passageways where mechanical handling equipment is used.
- Loose/unboxed materials which might fall from a pile are properly stacked by blocking, interlocking or limiting the height of the pile to prevent falling hazards.

- Bags, containers, bundles, etc. are stored in tiers that are stacked, blocked, interlocked and limited in height so that they are stable and secure to prevent sliding or collapse.
- Storage areas are kept free from accumulation of materials that could lead to tripping, fire, explosion or pest infestations.
- Excessive vegetation is removed from building entrances, work or traffic areas to prevent possible trip or fall hazards due to visual obstructions.
- Derail and/or bumper blocks are provided on spur railroad tracks where a rolling car could contact other cars being worked on and at entrances to buildings, work or traffic areas.
- Covers and/or guardrails are provided to protect personnel from the hazards of stair openings in floors, meter or equipment pits and similar hazards.
- Personnel use proper lifting techniques.
- Elevators and hoists for lifting materials/containers are properly used with adequate safe clearances, no obstructions, appropriate signals and directional warning signs.

Hazard Communication Safety

- All hazardous materials containers are properly labeled, indicating the chemical's identity, the manufacturer's name and address, and appropriate hazard warnings.
- There is an updated list of hazardous chemicals.
- The facility has a written program that covers hazard determination, including Material Safety Data Sheets (MSDSs), labeling and training.
- There is a system to check that each incoming chemical is accompanied by a MSDS.
- All employees are trained in the requirements of the hazard communication standard, the chemical hazards to which they are exposed, how to read and understand a MSDS and chemical labels, and on what precautions to take to prevent exposure.
- All employee training is documented.
- All outside contractors are given a complete list of chemical products, hazards and precautions.
- Procedures have been established to maintain and evaluate the effectiveness of the current program.
- Employees use proper personal protective equipment when handling chemicals.
- All chemicals are stored according to the manufacturer's recommendations and local or national fire codes.

Forklift Safety

- Powered industrial trucks (forklifts) meet the design and construction requirements established in American National Standard for Powered Industrial Trucks, Part II ANSI B56.1-1969.
- Written approval from the truck manufacturer has been obtained for any modifications or additions that affect the capacity and safe operation of the vehicle.
- Capacity, operation and maintenance instruction plates, tags or decals are changed to specify any modifications or additions to the vehicle.
- Nameplates and markings are in place and maintained in a legible condition.
- Forklifts that are used in hazardous locations are appropriately marked/approved for such use.
- Battery charging is conducted only in designated areas.
- Appropriate facilities are provided for flushing and neutralizing spilled electrolytes, for fire extinguishing, for protecting charging apparatus from damage by trucks and for adequate ventilation to disperse fumes from gassing batteries.
- Conveyors, overhead hoists or equivalent materials handling equipment are provided for handling batteries.
- Reinstalled batteries are properly positioned and secured.

- Carboy tilters or siphons are used for handling electrolytes.
- Forklifts are properly positioned and brakes applied before workers start to change or charge batteries.
- Vent caps are properly functioning.
- Precautions are taken to prevent smoking, open flames, sparks or electric arcs in battery charging areas and during storage/changing of propane fuel tanks.
- Tools and other metallic objects are kept away from the top of uncovered batteries.
- Concentrations of noxious gases and fumes are kept below acceptable levels.
- Forklift operators are competent to operate a vehicle safely as demonstrated by successful completion of training and evaluation conducted and certified by persons with the knowledge, training and experience to train operators and evaluate their performance.
- The training program content includes all truck-related topics, workplace related topics and the requirements of 29 CFR 1910.178 for safe truck operation.
- Refresher training and evaluation is conducted whenever an operator has been observed operating the vehicle in an unsafe manner or has been involved in an accident or a near-miss incident.
- Refresher training and evaluation is conducted whenever an operator is assigned to drive a different type of truck or whenever a condition in the workplace changes in a manner that could affect safe operation of the truck.
- Evaluations of each operator's performance are conducted at least once every three years.
- Load engaging means are fully lowered, with controls neutralized, power shut off and brakes set when a forklift is left unattended.
- Operators maintain a safe distance from the edge of ramps or platforms while using forklifts on any elevated dock, platform or freight car.
- There is sufficient headroom for the forklift and operator under overhead installations, lights, pipes, sprinkler systems, etc.
- Overhead guards are provided in good condition to protect forklift operators from falling objects.
- Operators observe all traffic regulations, including authorized plant speed limits.
- Drivers are required to look in the direction of and keep a clear view of the path of travel.
- Operators run their trucks at a speed that will permit the vehicle to stop in a safe manner.
- Dock boards (bridge plates) are properly secured when loading or unloading from dock to truck.
- Stunt driving and horseplay are prohibited.
- All loads are stable, safely arranged and fit within the rated capacity of the truck.
- Operators fill fuel tanks only when the engine is not running.
- Replacement parts of trucks are equivalent in terms of safety with those used in the original design.
- Trucks are examined for safety before being placed into service and unsafe or defective trucks are removed from service.

Materials handling

Knowledge check

1. What is the minimum age requirement for the operation of a forklift, regardless of training?
    a) 16
    b) 18
    c) 21
    d) 25

2. A way to prevent materials handling hazards is to ____.
    a) refuse to allow personnel to ride equipment without a seat and seatbelt
    b) report all damaged equipment immediately
    c) operate within manufacturer's specifications
    d) All of these

3. Which of the following is a method for eliminating or reducing crane operation hazards?
    a) A competent person should visually inspect the crane once a year
    b) Never exceed the load limit by more than 10%
    c) Never move a load over co-workers
    d) All of these

4. Employers must comply with OSHA standards related to materials handling, including training and _____.
    a) equipment
    b) operations
    c) inspection
    d) all of these

Hazard communication

Hazard Communication Safety Data Sheets

The Hazard Communication Standard (HCS) requires chemical manufacturers, distributors, or importers to provide Safety Data Sheets (SDSs) (formerly known as Material Safety Data Sheets or MSDSs) to communicate the hazards of hazardous chemical products. The HCS requires new SDSs to be in a uniform format, and include the section numbers, the headings, and associated information under the headings below:

Section 1, Identification includes product identifier; manufacturer or distributor name, address, phone number; emergency phone number; recommended use; restrictions on use.

Section 2, Hazard(s) identification includes all hazards regarding the chemical; required label elements.

Section 3, Composition/information on ingredients includes information on chemical ingredients; trade secret claims.

Section 4, First-aid measures includes important symptoms/effects, acute, delayed; required treatment.

Section 5, Fire-fighting measures lists suitable extinguishing techniques, equipment; chemical hazards from fire.

Section 6, Accidental release measures lists emergency procedures; protective equipment; proper methods of containment and cleanup.

Section 7, Handling and storage lists precautions for safe handling and storage, including incompatibilities.

(Continued on other side)

For more information:

Occupational Safety and Health Administration

www.osha.gov (800) 321-OSHA (6742)

OSHA 3493-01R 2016

Hazard Communication Safety Data Sheets

Section 8, Exposure controls/personal protection lists OSHA's Permissible Exposure Limits (PELs); ACGIH Threshold Limit Values (TLVs); and any other exposure limit used or recommended by the chemical manufacturer, importer, or employer preparing the SDS where available as well as appropriate engineering controls; personal protective equipment (PPE).

Section 9, Physical and chemical properties lists the chemical's characteristics.

Section 10, Stability and reactivity lists chemical stability and possibility of hazardous reactions.

Section 11, Toxicological information includes routes of exposure; related symptoms, acute and chronic effects; numerical measures of toxicity.

Section 12, Ecological information*
Section 13, Disposal considerations*
Section 14, Transport information*
Section 15, Regulatory information*

Section 16, Other information, includes the date of preparation or last revision.

*Note: Since other Agencies regulate this information, OSHA will not be enforcing Sections 12 through 15 (29 CFR 1910.1200(g)(2)).

Employers must ensure that SDSs are readily accessible to employees.
See Appendix D of 29 CFR 1910.1200 for a detailed description of SDS contents.

For more information:

www.osha.gov (800) 321-OSHA (6742)

OSHA® QUICK CARD™

Hazard Communication Standard Labels

OSHA has updated the requirements for labeling of hazardous chemicals under its Hazard Communication Standard (HCS). All labels are required to have pictograms, a signal word, hazard and precautionary statements, the product identifier, and supplier identification. A sample revised HCS label, identifying the required label elements, is shown on the right. Supplemental information can also be provided on the label as needed.

SAMPLE LABEL

CODE _____
Product Name _____

Company Name _____
Street Address _____
City _____ **State** _____
Postal Code _____ **Country** _____
Emergency Phone Number _____

} Product Identifier

} Supplier Identification

Keep container tightly closed. Store in a cool, well-ventilated place that is locked.
Keep away from heat/sparks/open flame. No smoking.
Only use non-sparking tools.
Use explosion-proof electrical equipment.
Take precautionary measures against static discharge.
Ground and bond container and receiving equipment.
Do not breathe vapors.
Wear protective gloves.
Do not eat, drink or smoke when using this product.
Wash hands thoroughly after handling.
Dispose of in accordance with local, regional, national, international regulations as specified.

In Case of Fire: use dry chemical (BC) or Carbon Dioxide (CO_2) fire extinguisher to extinguish.

First Aid
If exposed call Poison Center.
If on skin (or hair): Take off immediately any contaminated clothing. Rinse skin with water.

Precautionary Statements

Hazard Pictograms

Signal Word
Danger

Highly flammable liquid and vapor.
May cause liver and kidney damage.
} Hazard Statements

Supplemental Information

Directions for Use
_____
_____

Fill weight: _____ Lot Number: _____
Gross weight: _____ Fill Date: _____
Expiration Date: _____

OSHA 3492-01R 2016

For more information:

OSHA® Occupational Safety and Health Administration

U.S. Department of Labor   www.osha.gov   (800) 321-OSHA (6742)

Hazard Communication Standard Pictogram

The Hazard Communication Standard (HCS) requires pictograms on labels to alert users of the chemical hazards to which they may be exposed. Each pictogram consists of a symbol on a white background framed within a red border and represents a distinct hazard(s). The pictogram on the label is determined by the chemical hazard classification.

HCS Pictograms and Hazards

Health Hazard	Flame	Exclamation Mark
• Carcinogen • Mutagenicity • Reproductive Toxicity • Respiratory Sensitizer • Target Organ Toxicity • Aspiration Toxicity	• Flammables • Pyrophorics • Self-Heating • Emits Flammable Gas • Self-Reactives • Organic Peroxides	• Irritant (skin and eye) • Skin Sensitizer • Acute Toxicity (harmful) • Narcotic Effects • Respiratory Tract Irritant • Hazardous to Ozone Layer (Non-Mandatory)
Gas Cylinder	**Corrosion**	**Exploding Bomb**
• Gases Under Pressure	• Skin Corrosion/Burns • Eye Damage • Corrosive to Metals	• Explosives • Self-Reactives • Organic Peroxides
Flame Over Circle	**Environment** (Non-Mandatory)	**Skull and Crossbones**
• Oxidizers	• Aquatic Toxicity	• Acute Toxicity (fatal or toxic)

For more information:

U.S. Department of Labor

Occupational Safety and Health Administration

www.osha.gov (800) 321-OSHA (6742)

OSHA 3491-01R 2016

Hazard communication

Knowledge check

1. A hazard communication program requires which of the following components?

    a) Written program

    b) SDS/Labeling

    c) Training

    d) All of the above

2. How many sections are required on an SDS?

    a) 11 sections

    b) 16 sections

    c) 4 sections

    d) As many as necessary to convey understanding

3. Which of the following statements is true of the pictograms on HCS labels?

    a) Pictograms on HCS labels are identical to those used on DOT transport labels and may have various background colors

    b) Consist of four bars that are color-coded as blue, red, yellow, and white to match hazard

    c) HCS pictograms are required and standardized red square-on-points with black hazard symbols and white backgrounds

4. Your right to understand is _____.

    a) not simply shown or told

    b) not simply given an SDS

    c) required at initial assignment/when thing change

    d) all of the above

Hazardous materials

OSHA FactSheet

Steps to an Effective Hazard Communication Program for Employers That Use Hazardous Chemicals

Employers that have hazardous chemicals in their workplaces are required by OSHA's Hazard Communication Standard (HCS), 29 CFR 1910.1200, to implement a hazard communication program. The program must include labels on containers of hazardous chemicals, safety data sheets (SDSs) for hazardous chemicals, and training for workers. Each employer must also describe in a written program how it will meet the requirements of the HCS in each of these areas.

Employers can implement an effective hazard communication program by following these six steps:

Step 1. Learn the Standard/Identify Responsible Staff

- Obtain a copy of OSHA's Hazard Communication Standard.
- Become familiar with its provisions.
- Make sure that someone has primary responsibility for coordinating implementation.
- Identify staff for particular activities (e.g., training).

You may obtain a copy of the Hazard Communication Standard on OSHA's hazard communication webpage at www.osha.gov/dsg/hazcom. The provisions of the standard that apply to employers using chemicals in their workplaces are found primarily in paragraphs (e) written hazard communication program; (f) labels and other forms of warning; (g) safety data sheets; and (h) employee information and training. It is important that you become familiar with these provisions to determine what is needed for compliance in your workplace.

In order to ensure that you have an effective hazard communication program, and address all of the necessary components, responsibility for implementation of hazard communication should be assigned to someone to coordinate. The person designated for overall program coordination should then identify staff to be responsible for particular activities, such as training.

Step 2. Prepare and Implement a Written Hazard Communication Program

- Prepare a written plan to indicate how hazard communication will be addressed in your facility.
- Prepare a list or inventory of all hazardous chemicals in the workplace.

Paragraph (e) of the standard requires employers to prepare and implement a written hazard communication program. This requirement is to help ensure that compliance with the standard is done in a systematic way, and that all elements are coordinated. The written program must indicate how you will address the requirements of paragraphs (f) labels and other forms of warning; (g) safety data sheets; and (h) employee information and training, in your workplace.

The written program also requires employers to maintain a list of the hazardous chemicals known to be present in the workplace. Using the product identifier (e.g., product name, common name, or chemical name) to prepare the list will make it easier for you to track the status of SDSs and labels of a particular hazardous chemical. Remember, the product identifier must be the same name that appears on the label and SDS of the hazardous chemical.

Step 3. Ensure Containers are Labeled
- Keep labels on shipped containers.
- Label workplace containers where required.

Chemical manufacturers and importers are required to provide labels on shipped containers with the following information: product identifier, signal word, pictograms, hazard statements, precautionary statements, and the name, address and phone number of the responsible party. Therefore, when an employer receives a hazardous chemical from a supplier, all of this information will be located together on the label; however, additional information may also appear.

As the employer, you are required to ensure that containers in the workplace are labeled. You may use the same label from the supplier or you may label workplace containers with alternatives, such as third party systems (e.g., National Fire Protection Association (NFPA) or Hazardous Materials Identification System (HMIS)) in addition to the other required information. Any container of hazardous chemicals in the workplace must at a minimum include the product identifier and general information concerning the hazards of the chemical. Whatever method you choose, your workers need to have access to the complete hazard information.

Step 4. Maintain Safety Data Sheets (SDSs)
- Maintain safety data sheets for each hazardous chemical in the workplace.
- Ensure that safety data sheets are readily accessible to employees.

Safety data sheets are the source of detailed information on a particular hazardous chemical. Employers must maintain copies of SDSs for all hazardous chemicals present in their workplaces. If you do not receive an SDS from your supplier automatically, you must request one. You also must ensure that SDSs are readily accessible to workers when they are in their work areas during their work shifts.

This accessibility may be accomplished in many different ways. You must decide what is appropriate for your particular workplace. Some employers keep the SDSs in a binder in a central location (e.g., outside of the safety office, in the pick-up truck on a construction site). Others, particularly in workplaces with large numbers of chemicals, provide access electronically. However, if SDSs are supplied electronically, there must be an adequate back-up system in place in the event of a power outage, equipment failure, or other emergency involving the primary electronic system. In addition, the employer must ensure that workers are trained on how to use the system to access SDSs and are able to obtain hard copies of the SDSs. In the event of a medical emergency, hard copy SDSs must be immediately available to medical personnel.

Step 5. Inform and Train Employees
- Train employees on the hazardous chemicals in their work area before initial assignment, and when new hazards are introduced.
- Include the requirements of the standard, hazards of chemicals, appropriate protective measures, and where and how to obtain additional information.

Paragraph (h) of the HCS requires that employers train employees on the hazardous chemicals in their work area before their initial assignment and when new hazards are introduced into the work area, and this training must be conducted in a manner and language that employees can understand. Workers must understand they are exposed to hazardous chemicals. They must know that labels and safety data sheets can provide them with information on the hazards of a chemical, and these items should be consulted when needed. In addition, workers must have a general understanding of what information is provided on labels and SDSs, and how to access them. They must also be aware of the protective measures available in their workplace, how to use or implement these measures, and whom they should contact if an issue arises.

Step 6. Evaluate and Reassess Your Program

- Review your hazard communication program periodically to make sure that it is still working and meeting its objectives.
- Revise your program as appropriate to address changed conditions in the workplace (e.g., new chemicals, new hazards, etc.).

Although the HCS does not require you to evaluate and reassess your hazard communication program, it must remain current and relevant for you and your employees. The best way to achieve that is to review your hazard communication program periodically to make sure that it is still working and meeting its objectives and to revise it as appropriate to address changed conditions in the workplace (e.g., new chemicals, new hazards, etc.).

Additional Information

See *Hazard Communication: Small Entity Compliance Guide for Employers That Use Hazardous Chemicals* for more detailed information on how to implement an effective hazard communication program. Additional information on the Hazard Communication Standard can be found on OSHA's Hazard Communication webpage at www.osha.gov/dsg/hazcom.

This is one in a series of informational fact sheets highlighting OSHA programs, policies or standards. It does not impose any new compliance requirements. For a comprehensive list of compliance requirements of OSHA standards or regulations, refer to Title 29 of the Code of Federal Regulations. This information will be made available to sensory-impaired individuals upon request. The voice phone is (202) 693-1999; teletypewriter (TTY) number: (877) 889-5627.

For assistance, contact us. We can help. It's confidential.

www.osha.gov (800) 321-OSHA (6742)

DSG FS-3696 03/2014

Activity: Workplace Hazard Analysis

Instructions: Complete the following Workplace Hazard Analysis worksheet, using the information provided in the Safety Data Sheet that follows it.

Anticipated or Potential Hazardous Materials (Check all that Apply):

☐ Gases ☐ Vapors ☐ Fumes ☐ Dusts ☐ Fibers ☐ Mists

Anticipated or Potential Physical Hazards (Check all that Apply):

☐ Fire ☐ Explosion ☐ Oxidizer ☐ Corrosive to Metal ☐ Gas under Pressure ☐ Self-Heating Substance

Anticipated or Potential Health Hazards (Check all that Apply):

☐ Toxic ☐ Skin/Eye Irritant ☐ Respiratory/Aspiration Hazard ☐ Carcinogen ☐ Reproductive Toxicity

☐ Confined or enclosed spaces (hazardous atmospheres).
☐ Contaminated soil conditions (hazardous atmospheres).
☐ Unsanitary conditions (poor housekeeping, poorly kept toilet facilities, etc.).
☐ Presence of hazardous materials (dangerous coatings on structures & metal containing alloys).
☐ The use of hazardous chemicals (gases, solvents, glues and concrete).
☐ The presence of residues left by degreasing agents, usually chlorinated hydrocarbons (chloroform and carbon tetrachloride).
☐ Older buildings and structures; unoccupied dwellings (fungi/mold, asbestos & lead).
☐ Homes built before 1978 – suspect to contain lead-based paint, according to the EPA.
☐ Extreme temperatures (hot & cold environments).
☐ Radiological exposures (nuclear power plants, antennas, hospitals, laboratories and the sun).
☐ Loud noise (use of tools and equipment).
☐ Hot work (welding and cutting).
☐ The presence of plant and/or animal wildlife (poisonous venom, feces, rabies…).
☐ Other: _____

Description of Health Hazard:

☐ Gas   ☐ Vapor   ☐ Fume   ☐ Dust/Fiber   ☐ Mist   ☐ Fungi (Mold)

☐ Radiation   ☐ Other

C.A.S # _____ Flash Point (FP) _____ Vapor/Gas Density _____ Lower Flammable Limit (LFL) _____

PEL: _____ TLV: _____ REL: _____ AL: _____ C: _____ STEL: _____

➤ Is there a safe alternative? Yes/No (If yes, describe: _____

➤ Is the work being performed by qualified people? Yes/No (List special training, certification and/or licensing required): _____

➤ Does the work involve entry into confined or enclosed spaces? Yes/No (if yes, follow confined space entry procedures).

➤ Is there a Safety Data Sheet (SDS) available on the job-site for all hazardous chemicals? Yes/No

➤ Are hazard controls being implemented in order of preference? Yes/No

1. Engineering: ventilation & wet methods.
2. Administrative; work practices, scheduling workers to minimize exposure, extended breaks, etc.
3. Personal Protective Equipment (PPE); respiratory and hearing protection, protection of face, hand, feet, eyes & whole body.

Health Hazard Route of Entry(s)

☐ Inhalation ☐ Ingestion ☐ Absorption ☐ Injection ☐ Other _____

Environmental & Personal Air Monitoring:

➤ Air monitoring does not measure you or what you are doing, but rather what you are exposed to on the job.

➤ Air monitoring must be done by a trained health professional (industrial hygienist or technician).

➤ Monitoring can be done by measuring the air in a fixed location in the work area (*area monitoring*) or by placing the monitoring equipment on individual workers and measuring the amount they are exposed to (*personal monitoring*).

Hazard Evaluation (*Employee Exposure Monitoring and/or Medical Surveillance*)

☐ Exposure Records: TWA: _____ C: _____ STEL: _____
(This information must be maintained by employer for 30 years.)

☐ Medical Records (List): _____
_____
_____

(This information must be maintained by employer for duration of employment, plus 30 years.)

Engineering Controls (Select engineering controls to be implemented):

- ☐ Dust suppression (wet methods): _____
- ☐ Dust collection systems (vacuum): _____
- ☐ General (dilution) ventilation; works best when air contaminants are widely disbursed through the area.
- ☐ Local (exhaust) ventilation system; works well when air contaminants are generated at a single source.

Describe mechanical ventilation system used: _____

General (Dilution) Ventilation...

Forces fresh air into an area and dilutes contaminants; this allows air to move through a space which ensures a fresh continual supply.

Local (Exhaust) Ventilation...

Removes contaminated air at its source; this prevents harmful dust, fumes & mists from contaminating the breathing air of the worker.

If no engineering controls are being implemented, person authorizing the non-use of engineering controls:

Name: _____   Date: _____   Reason (explain): _____

61

Administrative Controls (used with personal protective equipment):

- ☐ Gather all specialty equipment, including, ventilators, warning signs, personal protective equipment, etc. (list all specialty equipment needed for job): _____
- ☐ Operations that involve toxic substances are scheduled at times when other workers are not present? Yes/No (describe): _____
- ☐ Work is isolated to just a few protected employees; signs posted and controlled access zones established? Yes/No (describe): _____
- ☐ Employees are rotated in and out of jobs to minimize exposure? Yes/No (describe): _____
- ☐ Employees removed from working around hazardous substances once they have reached a predetermined level of exposure? Yes/No (describe): _____
- ☐ Are hot and cold work environments considered? Yes/No (describe): _____
- ☐ Employees trained on proper housekeeping & good personal hygiene? Yes/No
- ☐ Employees trained on the proper procedures that minimize exposures? Yes/No
- ☐ Employees trained on how to inspect and maintain process and equipment on a regular basis? Yes/No
- ☐ No eating, drinking, smoking, chewing tobacco or gum, and applying cosmetics in hazardous areas? Yes/No

Controlling a hazard at its source is the best way to protect workers. However, when engineering, work practices and administrative controls are not feasible* or do not provide sufficient protection, employers must provide ***personal protective equipment (PPE)*** to the employee and ensure its proper use.

Description of personal protective equipment being used: ☐ Eye/Face Protection ☐ Foot Protection
☐ Body Protection ☐ Gloves ☐ Respirator ☐ Other _____

- ☐ Is the device approved? Yes/No (describe): _____
- ☐ Is the device appropriate for the type of hazard? Yes/No (explain): _____
- ☐ Is the worker wearing the device properly trained to understand the use, limitations and care instructions of the device? Yes/No (explain):
- ☐ Does the material have sufficient strength to withstand the environment? Yes/No (explain):
- ☐ Will the material withstand repeated use after contamination and decontamination? Yes/No (explain):
- ☐ Is the material flexible or pliable enough to allow end users to perform needed tasks? Yes/No (describe):
- ☐ Will the material maintain its protective integrity and flexibility under hot and cold extremes? Yes/No (explain):

Safety Data Sheet
Revision Date: 01/17/18
www.restek.com

2 Letter ISO country code/language code: US/EN

1. IDENTIFICATION

Catalog Number / Product Name:	32228 / Heptachlor Standard
Company:	Restek Corporation
Address:	110 Benner Circle
	Bellefonte, Pa. 16823
Phone#:	814-353-1300
Fax#:	814-353-1309
Emergency#:	800-424-9300 (CHEMTREC)
	703-527-3887 (Outside the US)
Email:	www.restek.com
Revision Number:	8
Intended use:	For Laboratory use only

2. HAZARD(S)IDENTIFICATION

Emergency Overview:

GHS Hazard Symbols:

GHS Classification:
Specific Target Organ Systemic Toxicity (STOT) - Single Exposure Category 1
Flammable Liquid Category 2
Carcinogenicity Category 2
Acute Toxicity - Dermal Category 3
Acute Toxicity - Oral Category 3

GHS Signal Word: Danger

GHS Hazard:
Highly flammable liquid and vapour.
Toxic if swallowed or in contact with skin.
Suspected of causing cancer.
Causes damage to organs.

GHS Precautions:

Safety Precautions:
Obtain special instructions before use.
Do not handle until all safety precautions have been read and understood.
Keep away from heat/sparks/open flames/hot surfaces. – No smoking.
Keep container tightly closed.
Ground/bond container and receiving equipment.
Use explosion-proof electrical/ventilation and lighting equipment.
Use only non-sparking tools.
Take precautionary measures against static discharge.
Do not breathe dust/fume/gas/mist/vapours/spray.
Wash hands and skin thoroughly after handling.
Do not eat, drink or smoke when using this product.
Wear protective gloves/protective clothing/eye protection/face protection.

First Aid Measures:
IF SWALLOWED: Immediately call a POISON CENTER/doctor/....
IF ON SKIN: Wash with plenty of soap and water.
IF ON SKIN (or hair): Remove/Take off immediately all contaminated clothing. Rinse skin with water/shower.
IF exposed: Call a POISON CENTER or doctor/physician.
IF exposed or concerned: Get medical advice/attention.
Call a POISON CENTER or doctor/physician if you feel unwell.
Specific treatment see section 4.

	Rinse mouth. Take off immediately all contaminated clothing and wash it before reuse. In case of fire: Use extinguishing media in section 5 for extinction.
Storage:	Keep container tightly closed. Store in a well-ventilated place. Keep cool. Store locked up.
Disposal:	Dispose of contents/container according to section 13 of the SDS.
Single Exposure Target Organs:	Specific target organ toxicity - Single exposure - STOT SE 1: H370 Causes damage to organs. (C >= 10 %; No information to prove exclusion of certain routes of exposure); Specific target organ toxicity - Single exposure - STOT SE 2: H371 May cause damage to organs. (3 % <= C <10 %; Concentration limits for acute toxicity cannot be translated into GHS from the DSD especially when minimum classifications are given)
Repeated Exposure Target Organs:	Specific target organ toxicity - Repeated exposure - STOT RE 2: H373 May cause damage to organs through prolonged or repeated exposure. (Minimum classification, No information to prove exclusion of certain routes of exposure)

3. COMPOSITION / INFORMATION ON INGREDIENT

Chemical Name	CAS #	EINEC #	% Composition
methanol	67-56-1	200-659-6	99.9
heptachlor	76-44-8	200-962-3	0.1

4. FIRST-AID MEASURES

Inhalation:	Remove to fresh air. If breathing is difficult, have a trained individual administer oxygen. If not breathing, give artificial respiration and have a trained individual administer oxygen. Get medical attention immediately
Eyes:	Flush eyes with plenty of water for at least 20 minutes retracting eyelids often. Tilt the head to prevent chemical from transferring to the uncontaminated eye. Get immediate medical attention.
Skin Contact:	Wash with soap and water. Remove contaminated clothing and launder. Get medical attention if irritation develops or persists.
Ingestion:	Do not induce vomiting and seek medical attention immediately. Drink two glasses of water or milk to dilute. Provide medical care provider with this SDS.

5. FIRE- FIGHTING MEASURES

Extinguishing Media:	Use alcohol resistant foam, carbon dioxide, or dry chemical extinguishing agents. Water may be ineffective but water spray can be used extinguish a fire if swept across the base of the flames. Water can absorb heat and keep exposed material from being damaged by fire.
Fire and/or Explosion Hazards:	Vapors may be ignited by sparks, flames or other sources of ignition if material is above the flash point giving rise to a fire (Class B). Vapors are heavier than air and may travel to a source of ignition and flash back.
Fire Fighting Methods and Protection:	Do not enter fire area without proper protection including self-contained breathing apparatus and full protective equipment. Fight fire from a safe distance and a protected location due to the potential of hazardous vapors and decomposition products. Flammable component(s) of this material may be lighter than water and burn while floating on the surface.
Hazardous Combustion Products:	Carbon dioxide, Carbon monoxide

6. ACCIDENTAL RELEASE MEASURES

Personal Precautions and Equipment:	Exposure to the spilled material may be severely irritating or toxic. Follow personal protective equipment recommendations found in Section 8 of this SDS. Personal protective equipment needs must be evaluated based on information provided on this sheet and the special circumstances created by the spill including; the material spilled, the quantity of the spill, the area in which the spill occurred, and the expertise of employees in the area responding to the spill. Never exceed any occupational exposure limits.
Methods for Clean-up:	Prevent the spread of any spill to minimize harm to human health and the environment if safe to do so. Wear complete and proper personal protective equipment following the recommendation of Section 8 at a

minimum. Dike with suitable absorbent material like granulated clay. Gather and store in a sealed container pending a waste disposal evaluation.

7. HANDLING AND STORAGE

Handling Technical Measures and Precautions:	Toxic or severely irritating material. Avoid contacting and avoid breathing the material. Use only in a well ventilated area. Use spark-proof tools and explosion-proof equipment
Storage Technical Measures and Conditions:	Store in a cool dry ventilated location. Isolate from incompatible materials and conditions. Keep container(s) closed. Keep away from sources of ignition

8. EXPOSURE CONTROLS / PERSONAL PROTECTION

United States:

Chemical Name	CAS No.	IDLH	ACGIH STEL	ACGIH TLV-TWA	OSHA Exposure Limit
methanol	67-56-1	6000 ppm IDLH	250 ppm STEL	200 ppm TWA	200 ppm TWA; 260 mg/m3 TWA
heptachlor	76-44-8	35 mg/m3 IDLH	None Known	0.05 mg/m3 TWA	0.5 mg/m3 TWA

Personal Protection:

Engineering Measures:	Local exhaust ventilation is recommended when generating excessive levels of vapours from handling or thermal processing.
Respiratory Protection:	Respiratory protection may be required to avoid overexposure when handling this product. General or local exhaust ventilation is the preferred means of protection. Use a respirator if general room ventilation is not available or sufficient to eliminate symptoms. If an exposure limit is exceeded or if an operator is experiencing symptoms of inhalation overexposure as explained in Section 3, provide respiratory protection.
Eye Protection:	Wear chemically resistant safety glasses with side shields when handling this product. Do not wear contact lenses.
Skin Protection:	Wear protective gloves. Inspect gloves for chemical break-through and replace at regular intervals. Clean protective equipment regularly. Wash hands and other exposed areas with mild soap and water before eating, drinking, and when leaving work

9. PHYSICAL AND CHEMICAL PROPERTIES

Appearance, color:	No data available
Odor:	Mild
Physical State:	No data available
pH:	Not applicable
Vapor Pressure:	No data available
Vapor Density:	1.1 (air = 1)
Boiling Point (°C):	64.7 °C at 760 mmHg (HSDB)
Melting Point (°C):	-98 °C
Flash Point (°F):	52
Flammability:	Highly Flammable
Upper Flammable/Explosive Limit, % in air:	36
Lower Flammable/Explosive Limit, % in air:	6
Autoignition Temperature (°C):	464 deg C
Decomposition Temperature (°C):	No data available
Specific Gravity:	0.791 - 0.792 g/cm3 at 20 °C
Evaporation Rate:	No data available
Odor Threshold:	No data available
Solubility:	Moderate; 50-99%
Partition Coefficient: n-octanol in water:	No data available
VOC % by weight:	0
Molecular Weight:	32.04

10. STABILITY AND REACTIVITY

Stability:	Stable under normal conditions.
Conditions to Avoid:	None known.
Materials to Avoid / Chemical Incompatiability:	Strong oxidizing agents
Hazardous Decomposition Products:	Carbon dioxide Carbon monoxide

11. TOXICOLOGICAL INFORMATION

Routes of Entry:	Inhalation, Skin Contact, Eye Contact, Ingestion
Target Organs Potentially Affected By Exposure:	Eyes, Central nervous system stimulation, Skin, GI Tract, Respiratory Tract
Chemical Interactions That Change Toxicity:	None Known

Immediate (Acute) Health Effects by Route of Exposure:

Inhalation Irritation:	Can cause moderate respiratory irritation, dizziness, weakness, fatigue, nausea and headache.
Inhalation Toxicity:	Harmful! Can cause systemic damage (see "Target Organs)Methanol can cause central nervous system depression and overexposure can cause damage to the optic nerve resulting in visual impairment or blindness.
Skin Contact:	Can cause moderate skin irritation, defatting, and dermatitis. Not likely to cause permanent damage.
Eye Contact:	Can cause moderate irritation, tearing and reddening, but not likely to permanently injure eye tissue.
Ingestion Irritation:	Irritating to mouth, throat, and stomach. Can cause abdominal discomfort, nausea, vomiting and diarrhea.Highly toxic and may be fatal if swallowed.
Ingestion Toxicity:	Toxic if swallowed. May cause target organ failure and/or death.May be fatal if swallowed.

Long-Term (Chronic) Health Effects:

Carcinogenicity:	Contains a probable or known human carcinogen.
Reproductive and Developmental Toxicity:	No data available to indicate product or any components present at greater than 0.1% may cause birth defects.
Inhalation:	Upon prolonged and/or repeated exposure, can cause moderate respiratory irritation, dizziness, weakness, fatigue, nausea and headache.Harmful! Can cause systemic damage upon prolonged and/or repeated exposure (see "Target Organs)
Skin Contact:	Upon prolonged or repeated contact, can cause moderate skin irritation, defatting, and dermatitis. Not likely to cause permanent damage.
Ingestion:	Toxic if swallowed. May cause target organ failure and/or death.

Component Toxicological Data:
NIOSH:

Chemical Name	CAS No.	LD50/LC50
Heptachlor	76-44-8	Dermal LD50 Rabbit 780 mg/kg
Methanol	67-56-1	Inhalation LC50 Rat 22500 ppm 8 h

Component Carcinogenic Data:
OSHA:

Chemical Name	CAS No.	
Heptachlor	76-44-8	Present

ACGIH:

Chemical Name	CAS No.	
Heptachlor	76-44-8	A3 - Confirmed Animal Carcinogen with Unknown Relevance to Humans

NIOSH:

Chemical Name	CAS No.	
Heptachlor	76-44-8	potential occupational carcinogen

NTP:

Chemical Name	CAS No.
No data available	

IARC:

Chemical Name	CAS No.	Group No.
Monograph 79 [2001]; Monograph 53 [1991]; Supplement 7 [1987]	76-44-8	Group 2B

32228 / Heptachlor Standard

12. ECOLOGICAL INFORMATION

Overview:	Moderate ecological hazard. This product may be dangerous to plants and/or wildlife.
Mobility:	No data
Persistence:	No data
Bioaccumulation:	No data
Degradability:	Biodegrades slowly.
Ecological Toxicity Data:	No data available

13. DISPOSAL CONSIDERATIONS

Waste Description of Spent Product:	Spent or discarded material is a hazardous waste. Mixing spent or discarded material with other materials may render the mixture hazardous. Perform a hazardous waste determination on mixtures.
Disposal Methods:	Dispose of by incineration following Federal, State, Local, or Provincial regulations.
Waste Disposal of Packaging:	Comply with all Local, State, Federal, and Provincial Environmental Regulations.

14. TRANSPORTATION INFORMATION

United States:

DOT Proper Shipping Name:	Methanol
UN Number:	UN1230
Hazard Class:	3
Packing Group:	II

International:

IATA Proper Shipping Name:	Methanol
UN Number:	UN1230
Hazard Class:	3(6.1)
Packing Group:	II

Marine Pollutant: No

Chemical Name	CAS#	Marine Pollutant	Severe Marine Pollutant
No data available			

15. REGULATORY INFORMATION

United States:

Chemical Name	CAS#	CERCLA	SARA 313	SARA EHS 313	TSCA
methanol	67-56-1	X	X	-	X
heptachlor	76-44-8	X	X	-	-

The following chemicals are listed on CA Prop 65:

Chemical Name	CAS #	Regulation
Heptachlor	76-44-8	Prop 65 Cancer
Heptachlor	76-44-8	Prop 65 Devolop Tox
Methanol	67-56-1	Prop 65 Devolop Tox

State Right To Know Listing:

Chemical Name	CAS#	New Jersey	Massachusetts	Pennsylvania	California
methanol	67-56-1	X	X	X	X
heptachlor	76-44-8	X	X	X	X

16. OTHER INFORMATION

Prior Version Date:	12/13/16
Other Information:	Any changes to the SDS compared to previous versions are marked by a vertical line in front of the concerned paragraph.
References:	No data available
Disclaimer:	Restek Corporation provides the descriptions, data and information contained

32228 / Heptachlor Standard

herein in good faith but makes no representation as to its comprehensiveness or accuracy. It is provided for your guidance only. Because many factors may affect processing or application/use, Restek Corporation recommends you perform an assessment to determine the suitability of a product for your particular purpose prior to use. No warranties of any kind, either expressed or implied, including fitness for a particular purpose, are made regarding products described, data or information set forth. In no case shall the descriptions, information, or data provided be considered a part of our terms and conditions of sale. Further, the descriptions, data and information furnished hereunder are given gratis. No obligation or liability for the description, data and information given are assumed. All such being given and accepted at your risk.

Hazardous materials

Knowledge check

1. The most common route of entry by which hazardous materials are introduced into the body is ____.

   a) inhalation

   b) absorption

   c) ingestion

   d) injection

2. Flammability is which type of hazard?

   a) Carcinogenic

   b) Health

   c) Physical

   d) Mutagenic

3. Which of the following hazards is an example of a physical hazard?

   a) Oxidizer

   b) Exposure to carcinogen

   c) Chronic toxicity

   d) Acute toxicity

4. Which of the following hazards is an example of a health hazard?

   a) Fire hazard

   b) Acute toxicity

   c) Explosive

   d) High pressure

5. Which of the following is the preferred order of controlling hazards, or "hierarchy of controls," for hazardous materials?

   a) PPE, Administrative Controls, Engineering Controls, Elimination

   b) Administrative Controls, Engineering Controls, Elimination, PPE

   c) Engineering Controls, Elimination, PPE, Administrative Controls

   d) Elimination, Engineering Controls, Administrative Controls, PPE

6. When transferring a flammable liquid from one container to another, the containers should be ____ to prevent static electricity from creating a fire hazard.

   a) ventilated or pressurized

   b) ventilated and pressurized

   c) bonded or grounded

   d) bonded and grounded

7. Which of the following hazard controls is an example of an engineering control?

   a) Enclosing an operation to prevent contact with the hazardous material

   b) Training employees on the proper handling and storage of a hazardous material

   c) Implementing a procedure for the proper use of a hazardous material

   d) Requiring personal protective equipment to be worn when working with a hazardous material

Walking and working surfaces, including fall protection

OSHA FactSheet

OSHA's Final Rule to Update, Align, and Provide Greater Flexibility in its General Industry Walking-Working Surfaces and Fall Protection Standards

Background

Falls from heights and on the same level (a working surface) are among the leading causes of serious work-related injuries and deaths. OSHA estimates that, on average, approximately 202,066 serious (lost-workday) injuries and 345 fatalities occur annually among workers directly affected by the final standard. OSHA's final rule on Walking-Working Surfaces and Personal Fall Protection Systems better protects workers in general industry from these hazards by updating and clarifying standards and adding training and inspection requirements. The rule affects a wide range of workers, from window washers to chimney sweeps. It does not change construction or agricultural standards.

The rule incorporates advances in technology, industry best practices, and national consensus standards to provide effective and cost-efficient worker protection. Specifically, the rule updates general industry standards addressing slip, trip, and fall hazards (subpart D), and adds requirements for personal fall protection systems (subpart I).

OSHA estimates this rule will prevent 29 fatalities and 5,842 lost-workday injuries every year.

The rule benefits employers by providing greater flexibility in choosing a fall protection system. For example, it eliminates the existing mandate to use guardrails as a primary fall protection method and allows employers to choose from accepted fall protection systems they believe will work best in a particular situation — an approach that has been successful in the construction industry since 1994. In addition, employers will be able to use non-conventional fall protection in certain situations, such as designated areas on low-slope roofs.

As much as possible, OSHA aligned fall protection requirements for general industry with those for construction, easing compliance for employers who perform both types of activities.

For example, the final rule replaces the outdated general industry scaffold standards with a requirement that employers comply with OSHA's construction scaffold standards.

The rule phases out a 1993 exception for the outdoor advertising industry that allows "qualified climbers" to forego fall protection. At least three workers have fallen from fixed ladders under this exception. One of them died. The final rule phases in the fixed ladder fall protection requirements for employers in outdoor advertising.

Fall Protection Options

The rule requires employers to protect workers from fall hazards along unprotected sides or edges that are at least 4 feet above a lower level. It also sets requirements for fall protection in specific situations, such as hoist areas, runways, areas above dangerous equipment, wall openings, repair pits, stairways, scaffolds, and slaughtering platforms. And it establishes requirements for the performance, inspection, use, and maintenance of personal fall protection systems.

OSHA defines fall protection as "any equipment, device, or system that prevents a worker from falling from an elevation or mitigates the effect of such a fall." Under the final rule, employers may choose from the following fall protection options:

- **Guardrail System** – A barrier erected along an unprotected or exposed side, edge, or other area of a walking-working surface to prevent workers from falling to a lower level.
- **Safety Net System** – A horizontal or semi-horizontal, cantilever-style barrier that uses a netting system to stop falling workers before they make contact with a lower level or obstruction.
- **Personal Fall Arrest System** – A system that

arrests/stops a fall before the worker contacts a lower level. Consists of a body harness, anchorage, and connector, and may include a lanyard, deceleration device, lifeline, or a suitable combination. Like OSHA's construction standards, the final rule prohibits the use of body belts as part of a personal fall arrest system.
- **Positioning System** – A system of equipment and connectors that, when used with a body harness or body belt, allows a worker to be supported on an elevated vertical surface, such as a wall or window sill, and work with both hands free.
- **Travel Restraint System** – A combination of an anchorage, anchorage connector, lanyard (or other means of connection), and body support to eliminate the possibility of a worker going over the unprotected edge or side of a walking-working surface.
- **Ladder Safety System** – A system attached to a fixed ladder designed to eliminate or reduce the possibility of a worker falling off the ladder. A ladder safety system usually consists of a carrier, safety sleeve, lanyard, connectors, and body harness. Cages and wells are not considered ladder safety systems.

Rope Descent Systems

The rule codifies a 1991 OSHA memorandum that permits employers to use Rope Descent Systems (RDS), which consist of a roof anchorage, support rope, descent device, carabiners or shackles, and a chair or seatboard. These systems are widely used throughout the country to perform elevated work, such as window washing.

The rule adds a 300-foot height limit for the use of RDS. It also requires building owners to affirm in writing that permanent building anchorages used for RDS have been tested, certified, and maintained as capable of supporting 5,000 pounds for each worker attached. This mirrors the requirement in OSHA's Powered Platforms standard.

Ladder Safety Requirements

Falls from ladders account for 20 percent of all fatal and lost work-day injuries in general industry. The new rule includes requirements to protect workers from falling off fixed and portable ladders as well as mobile ladder stands and platforms. (The ladder requirements do not apply to ladders used in emergency operations or ladders that are an integral part of or designed into a machine or piece of equipment).

In general, ladders must be capable of supporting their maximum intended load, while mobile ladder stands and platforms must be capable of supporting four times their maximum intended load. Each ladder must be inspected before initial use in a work shift to identify defects that could cause injury.

Fixed Ladders – Fixed ladders are permanently attached to a structure, building, or equipment. These include individual-rung ladders, but not ship stairs, step bolts, or manhole steps. The new rule phases in a requirement for employers to have ladder safety or personal fall arrest systems for fixed ladders that extend more than 24 feet, and phases out the use of cages or wells for fall protection under the following timeline: Starting in two years, all new fixed ladders and replacement ladder/ladder sections must have a ladder safety or personal fall protection system. For existing ladders, within two years, employers must install a cage, well, ladder safety system, or personal fall arrest system on fixed ladders that do not have any fall protection. Within 20 years, all ladders extending more than 24 feet must have a ladder safety or personal fall arrest system.

Portable Ladders – Portable ladders usually consist of side rails joined at intervals by steps, rungs, or cleats. They can be self-supporting or lean against a supporting structure. The final rule will be easier for employers and workers to understand and follow because it uses flexible performance-based language instead of detailed specification and design requirements. Under the revisions, employers must ensure that: rungs and steps are slip resistant; portable ladders used on slippery surfaces are secured and stabilized; portable ladders are not moved, shifted, or extended while a worker is on them; top steps and caps of stepladders are not used as steps; ladders are not fastened together to provide added length unless designed for such use; and ladders are not placed on boxes, barrels, or other unstable bases to obtain added height.

Training Requirements

The rule adds a requirement that employers ensure workers who use personal fall protection and work in other specified high hazard situations are trained, and retrained as necessary, about fall and equipment hazards, including fall protection systems. A qualified person must train these workers to correctly: identify and minimize fall hazards; use personal fall protection systems and rope descent systems; and maintain, inspect, and store equipment or systems used for fall protection.

When there is a change in workplace operations or equipment, or the employer believes that a worker would benefit from additional training based on a lack of knowledge or skill, then the worker must be retrained. The training must be provided in a language and vocabulary that workers understand.

Timeline

Most of the rule will become effective 60 days after it is published in the *Federal Register*, but some provisions have delayed effective dates, including:

- Ensuring exposed workers are trained on fall hazards (6 months),
- Ensuring workers who use equipment covered by the final rule are trained (6 months),
- Inspecting and certifying permanent anchorages for rope descent systems (1 year),
- Installing personal fall arrest or ladder safety systems on new fixed ladders over 24 feet and on replacement ladders/ladder sections, including fixed ladders on outdoor advertising structures (2 years),
- Ensuring existing fixed ladders over 24 feet, including those on outdoor advertising structures, are equipped with a cage, well, personal fall arrest system, or ladder safety system (2 years), and
- Replacing cages and wells (used as fall protection) with ladder safety or personal fall arrest systems on all fixed ladders over 24 feet (20 years).

Additional information

Additional information on OSHA's rule on walking-working surfaces and personal fall protection systems can be found at www.osha.gov/walking-working-surfaces. OSHA can provide extensive help through a variety of programs, including technical assistance about effective safety and health programs, workplace consultations, and training and education.

For more information on other safety-related issues impacting workers, to report an emergency, fatality, inpatient hospitalization, or to file a confidential complaint, contact your nearest OSHA office, visit www.osha.gov, or call OSHA at 1-800-321-OSHA (6742), TTY 1-877-889-5627.

This is one in a series of informational fact sheets highlighting OSHA programs, policies or standards. It does not impose any new compliance requirements. For a comprehensive list of compliance requirements of OSHA standards or regulations, refer to Title 29 of the Code of Federal Regulations. This information will be made available to sensory-impaired individuals upon request. The voice phone is (202) 693-1999; teletypewriter (TTY) number: (877) 889-5627.

For assistance, contact us. We can help. It's confidential.

www.osha.gov (800) 321-OSHA (6742)

DSG FS-3903 11/2016

U.S. Department of Labor

Walking and working surfaces, including fall protection

Knowledge check

1. Slips, trips, and falls make up what percent of all accidental deaths?

    a) 2%

    b) 15%

    c) 36%

    d) 50%

2. What is the easiest and most accurate way to use a portable ladder according to the manufacturer?

    a) Contact the manufacturer via cell phone

    b) Download the material from the internet

    c) Read and follow all warning labels and stickers

    d) Ask a fellow worker

3. When using a portable ladder to access another level, which statement is true?

    a) A step ladder may be used if long enough

    b) Portable ladders may never be used

    c) The ladder should be secured and extend 3 feet above the level you are accessing

    d) Carrying tools and materials is permitted

4. The maximum work level height of a free-standing scaffold's platform should never exceed ____ times the minimum base dimension.

    a) 2

    b) 3

    c) 4

    d) 5

5. Which best describes a safe scaffold?
    a) Placed on a firm foundation and is plumb and level
    b) Has proper access and is fully decked
    c) Has proper guardrail system
    d) All of the above

6. Scissor lifts rated for outdoor use are generally limited to wind speeds below ___.
    a) 28 MPH
    b) 50 MPH
    c) 60 MPH
    d) 75 MPH

7. The height of a proper guardrail system is ___ (+/− 3") from the walking/working surface.
    a) 30 inches
    b) 42 inches
    c) 60 inches
    d) None of the above

Fall protection

OSHA® QUICK CARD™

Fall Protection in General Industry

Falls are among the most common causes of serious work-related injuries and deaths. Employers must take measures in their workplaces to prevent employees from falling off overhead platforms, elevated work stations or into holes in the floor and walls.

Raised platform with protected guardrail.

To prevent employees from being injured from falls, employers must:

- Guard every floor hole into which a worker can accidentally walk by use of a railing and toeboard or a floor hole cover.
- Provide a guardrail and toeboard around every open-sided platform, floor or runway that is 4 feet or higher off the ground or next level.
- Regardless of height, if a worker can fall into or onto dangerous machines or equipment (such as a vat of acid or a conveyor belt), employers must provide guardrails and toeboards to prevent workers from falling and getting injured.
- Other means of fall protection that may be required on certain jobs include safety harness and line, safety nets, stair railings and handrails.

OSHA requires employers to:

- Provide working conditions that are free of known dangers.
- Keep floors in work areas in a clean and sanitary condition.
- Select and provide required personal protective equipment at no cost to workers.
- Train workers about job hazards in a language that they can understand.

You have a right to a safe workplace.
If you have questions about workplace safety and health, call OSHA at 1-800-321-6742.
It's confidential.
We can help!

For more complete information:

 **OSHA®** Occupational Safety and Health Administration

OSHA 3257-12-10R

U.S. Department of Labor
www.osha.gov   (800) 321-OSHA (6742)

Slips, Trips and Falls Fact Sheet

What causes slips, trips and falls?

Slips can occur when floors or other working surfaces become slippery due to wet or oily processes, floor cleaning, leaks, or from materials and debris left in walkways. Trips can occur due to uneven floor or working surfaces, protruding nails and boards, from stretched carpet or bunched floor mats intended to prevent slipping, from holes or depressions in working surfaces, and from step-risers on stairs that are not uniform in height. Both slips and trips can result in falls. In addition, falls can occur when ladders are not maintained properly, and when stairways and elevated working surfaces are not designed properly.

What types of injuries can occur?

According to OSHA, slips, trips and falls constitute the majority of general industry accidents and result in back injuries, strains and sprains, contusions, and fractures. Additionally, they cause 15 percent of all accidental deaths and are second only to motor vehicles as a cause of fatalities.

What can employers and employees do to prevent slips, trips and falls in the workplace?

- Where there are wet or oily processes, maintain drainage and provide false floors, platforms, nonslip mats or floor surfaces, or other dry standing places where practicable.
- Use no-skid waxes and surfaces coated with grit to create nonslip surfaces in slippery areas such as toilet and shower areas.
- Use slip-resistant footwear.
- Clean up floors and working surfaces promptly and frequently when they become wet.
- Use prudent housekeeping procedures such as cleaning only one side of a passageway at a time.
- Provide warning signs for wet floor areas.
- Provide floor plugs for equipment, so power cords need not run across pathways. Temporary electrical cords that must cross aisles should be taped or anchored to the floor.
- Aisles and passageways should be sufficiently wide for easy movement and should be kept clear at all times.

N.C. Department of Labor Occupational Safety and Health Division
1101 Mail Service Center, Raleigh, NC 27699-1101
(919) 807-2796 or 1-800-625-2267

- Re-lay or stretch carpets that bulge or have become bunched to prevent tripping hazards.
- Eliminate cluttered or obstructed work areas and keep file cabinet drawers closed.
- Provide good lighting for all halls and stairwells, especially during night hours.
- Make sure stairs have proper handrails, that treads and risers are maintained, and that treads have a slip-resistant surface.
- Instruct workers to use the handrail on stairs, to avoid undue speed, and to maintain an unobstructed view of the stairs ahead of them even if that means requesting help to manage a bulky load.
- Eliminate uneven floor surfaces.
- Make sure elevated storage and work surfaces have guardrails, toe boards and a permanent means of access.
- Make sure that floor drains, pits and other floor opening are covered or protected with guardrails.
- Use only properly maintained ladders with uniformly spaced rungs and nonslip safety feet to reach items. Do not use stools, chairs or boxes as substitutes for ladders.
- Train employees in the safe use of ladders.

Are there NCDOL standards for slips, trips and falls?

NCDOL requirements for the prevention of slips, trips and falls are contained in **29 CFR 1910, Subpart D, Walking-Working Surfaces**.

Where can I find additional information?

The NCDOL Library has fall prevention videos available under the "Falls" heading in the Video and DVD database. See NCDOL OSH Industry Guide # 41 A Guide to OSHA for Small Businesses in North Carolina, which contains checklists related to walking and working surfaces as well as other information. Also, see the Walking and Working Surfaces Subject Index on the OSHA Web site.

Fall protection

Knowledge check

1. What is the first line of defense when it comes to falls in the workplace?

    a) Control the fall itself once it occurs

    b) Eliminate the fall hazard completely

    c) With the fall hazard present, prevent the fall

    d) Use personal protective equipment

2. A worker is required to remove a section of guardrail in order to receive materials from a fork truck; which of the following provides the best protections to prevent a fall?

    a) Avoid the edge

    b) Use a personal fall arrest system

    c) Use a fall restraint system

    d) Use grab handles

3. A personal fall arrest system (PFAS) anchorage point must be capable of handling ____ pounds.

    a) 2,000

    b) 3,000

    c) 4,000

    d) 5,000

e)

Electrical

Electrical Safety

Electrical hazards can cause burns, shocks and electrocution (death).

- Assume that all overhead wires are energized at deadly voltages. Never assume that a wire is safe to touch even if it is down or appears to be insulated.

- Never touch a fallen overhead power line. Call the electric utility company to report fallen electrical lines.

- Stay at least 10 feet (3 meters) away from overhead wires during cleanup and other activities. If working at heights or handling long objects, survey the area before starting work for the presence of overhead wires.

- If an overhead wire falls across your vehicle while you are driving, stay inside the vehicle and continue to drive away from the line. If the engine stalls, do not leave your vehicle. Warn people not to touch the vehicle or the wire. Call or ask someone to call the local electric utility company and emergency services.

- Never operate electrical equipment while you are standing in water.

- Never repair electrical cords or equipment unless qualified and authorized.

- Have a qualified electrician inspect electrical equipment that has gotten wet before energizing it.

- If working in damp locations, inspect electric cords and equipment to ensure that they are in good condition and free of defects, and use a ground-fault circuit interrupter (GFCI).

- Always use caution when working near electricity.

For more information:

OSHA Occupational Safety and Health Administration
U.S. Department of Labor
www.osha.gov (800) 321-OSHA (6742)

OSHA 3294-04R-13

OSHA FactSheet

Working Safely with Electricity

Working with electricity can be dangerous. Engineers, linemen, electricians, and others work with electricity directly, including overhead lines, cable harnesses, and circuit assemblies. Office workers and salespeople work with electricity indirectly and may also be exposed to electrical hazards.

Generators

One of the common tools utilized following the loss of power are portable generators. Most generators are gasoline powered and use internal combustion engines to produce electricity. Carbon monoxide is a colorless and odorless gas produced during the operation of gasoline powered generators. When inhaled, the gas reduces your ability to utilize oxygen. Symptoms of carbon monoxide poisoning include headache, nausea and tiredness that can lead to unconsciousness and ultimately prove fatal.

- DO NOT bring a generator indoors. Be sure it is located outdoors in a location where the exhaust gases cannot enter a home or building. Good ventilation is the key.
- Be sure that the main circuit breaker is OFF and locked out prior to starting any generator. This will prevent inadvertent energization of power lines from back feed electrical energy from generators and help protect utility line workers from possible electrocution.
- Turn off generators and let them cool prior to refueling.

Power Lines

Overhead and buried power lines are especially hazardous because they carry extremely high voltage. Fatal electrocution is the main risk, but burns and falls are also hazards.

- Look for overhead power lines and buried power line indicators.
- Stay at least 10 feet away from overhead power lines and assume they are energized.
- De-energize and ground lines when working near them.
- Use non-conductive wood or fiberglass ladders when working near power lines.

Extension Cords

Normal wear on cords can loosen or expose wires. Cords that are not 3-wire type, not designed for hard-usage, or that have been modified, increase your risk of contacting electrical current.

- Use only equipment that is approved to meet OSHA standards.
- Do not modify cords or use them incorrectly.
- Use factory-assembled cord sets and only extension cords that are 3-wire type.
- Use only cords, connection devices, and fittings that are equipped with strain relief.
- Remove cords from receptacles by pulling on the plugs, not the cords.

Equipment

Due to the dynamic, rugged nature of construction work, normal use of electrical equipment causes wear and tear that results in insulation breaks, short-circuits, and exposed wires. If there is no ground-fault protection, it can cause a ground-fault that sends current through the worker's body.

- Use ground-fault circuit interrupters (GFCIs) on all 120-volt, single-phase, 15- and 20-ampere receptacles, or have an assured equipment grounding conductor program (AEGCP).
- Use double-insulated tools and equipment, distinctively marked.
- Visually inspect all electrical equipment before use. Remove from service any equipment with frayed cords, missing ground prongs, cracked tool casings, etc.

Electrical Incidents

If the power supply to the electrical equipment is not grounded or the path has been broken, fault current may travel through a worker's body, causing electrical burns or death. Even when the power system is properly grounded, electrical equipment can instantly change from safe to hazardous because of extreme conditions and rough treatment.

- Visually inspect electrical equipment before use. Take any defective equipment out of service.
- Ground all power supply systems, electrical circuits, and electrical equipment.
- Frequently inspect electrical systems to insure that the path to ground is continuous.
- Do not remove ground prongs from cord- and plug-connected equipment or extension cords.
- Use double-insulated tools and ground all exposed metal parts of equipment.
- Avoid standing in wet areas when using portable electrical power tools.

This is one in a series of informational fact sheets highlighting OSHA programs, policies or standards. It does not impose any new compliance requirements. For a comprehensive list of compliance requirements of OSHA standards or regulations, refer to Title 29 of the Code of Federal Regulations. This information will be made available to sensory impaired individuals upon request. The voice phone is (202) 693-1999; teletypewriter (TTY) number: (877) 889-5627.

Think Safety!
For more complete information:

OSHA Occupational Safety and Health Administration

U.S. Department of Labor
www.osha.gov
(800) 321-OSHA

Electrical

Knowledge check

1. What is electricity?

    a) The movement of atoms within an object

    b) The movement of free electrons between atoms

    c) Solid mass

    d) Movement within the nucleus of an atom

2. "Electrocution" means ____.

    a) received a mild electrical shock

    b) killed by electrical shock

    c) exposed to electrical current

    d) any accident involving electricity

3. Arc flash/arc blast can reach maximum temperatures up to 350°F.

    a) True

    b) False

4. Which gauge of wire will carry the most current?

    a) 14 gauge

    b) 12 gauge

    c) 10 gauge

    d) 00 gauge

5. What does GFCI stand for?

    a) Ground Flexible Conduit Insulator

    b) Ground Flow Current Interceptor

    c) Ground Fault Circuit Interrupter

    d) Ground Floor Connection Intersector

6. Which of the following is a safe practice?

    a) Carrying power tool by the cord

    b) Holding fingers on switch button while carrying a plugged-in tool

    c) Keeping cords away from heat, oil, and sharp edges

    d) Yanking cord to disconnect plug from outlet

7. Who is responsible for ensuring that overhead power lines are de-energized?

    a) Power company

    b) Employer

    c) Employee

    d) Municipality

Machine guarding

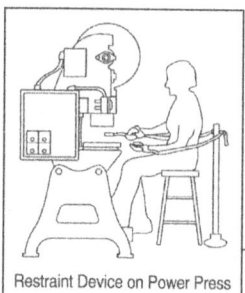
Restraint Device on Power Press

OSHA FACT Sheet

Amputations

What are the sources of amputations in the workplace?

Amputations are some of the most serious and debilitating workplace injuries. They are widespread and involve a variety of activities and equipment. Amputations occur most often when workers operate unguarded or inadequately safeguarded mechanical power presses, power press brakes, powered and non-powered conveyors, printing presses, roll-forming and roll-bending machines, food slicers, meat grinders, meat-cutting band saws, drill presses, and milling machines as well as shears, grinders, and slitters. These injuries also happen during materials handling activities and when using forklifts and doors as well as trash compactors and powered and non-powered hand tools. Besides normal operation, the following activities involving stationary machines also expose workers to potential amputation hazards: setting-up, threading, preparing, adjusting, cleaning, lubricating, and maintaining machines as well as clearing jams.

What types of machine components are hazardous?

The following types of mechanical components present amputation hazards:

- **Point of operation**—the area of a machine where it performs work on material.
- **Power-transmission apparatuses**—flywheels, pulleys, belts, chains, couplings, spindles, cams, and gears in addition to connecting rods and other machine components that transmit energy.
- **Other moving parts**—machine components that move during machine operation such as reciprocating, rotating, and transverse moving parts as well as auxiliary machine parts.

What kinds of mechanical motion are hazardous?

All mechanical motion is potentially hazardous. In addition to in-running nip points ("pinch points")—which occur when two parts move together and at least one moves in a rotary or circular motion that gears, rollers, belt drives, and pulleys generate—the following are the most common types of hazardous mechanical motion:

- **Rotating**—circular movement of couplings, cams, clutches, flywheels, and spindles as well as shaft ends and rotating collars that may grip clothing or otherwise force a body part into a dangerous location.
- **Reciprocating**—back-and-forth or up-and-down action that may strike or entrap a worker between a moving part and a fixed object.
- **Transversing**—movement in a straight, continuous line that may strike or catch a worker in a pinch or shear point created between the moving part and a fixed object.
- **Cutting**—action generated during sawing, boring, drilling, milling, slicing, and slitting.
- **Punching**—motion resulting when a machine moves a slide (ram) to stamp or blank metal or other material.
- **Shearing**—movement of a powered slide or knife during metal trimming or shearing.
- **Bending**—action occurring when power is applied to a slide to draw or form metal or other materials.

Are there any OSHA standards that cover amputation hazards in the workplace?

Yes. The Occupational Safety and Health Administration (OSHA) has the following standards in *Title 29 of the Code of Federal Regulations* (*CFR*) to protect workers from amputations in the workplace:

- 29 *CFR* Part 1910 Subparts O and P cover machinery and machine guarding.
- 29 *CFR* 1926 Subpart I covers hand tools and powered tools.
- 29 *CFR* Part 1928 Subpart D covers agricultural equipment.
- 29 *CFR* Part 1915 Subparts C, H, and J; 29 *CFR* Part 1917 Subparts B, C, and G; and 29 *CFR* Part 1918 Subparts F, G, and H cover maritime operations.

What can employers do to help protect workers from amputations?

You should be able to recognize, identify, manage, and control amputation hazards commonly found in the workplace such as those caused by mechanical components of machinery, the mechanical motion that occurs in or near these components, and the activities that workers perform during mechanical operation.

Work practices, employee training, and administrative controls can help prevent and control amputation hazards. Machine safeguarding with the following equipment is the best way to control amputations caused by stationary machinery:

- **Guards** provide physical barriers that prevent access to hazardous areas. They should be secure and strong, and workers should not be able to bypass, remove, or tamper with them. Guards should not obstruct the operator's view or prevent employees from working.

- **Devices** help prevent contact with points of operation and may replace or supplement guards. Devices can interrupt the normal cycle of the machine when the operator's hands are at the point of operation, prevent the operator from reaching into the point of operation, or withdraw the operator's hands if they approach the point of operation when the machine cycles. They must allow safe lubrication and maintenance and not create hazards or interfere with normal machine operation. In addition, they should be secure, tamper-resistant, and durable.

You are responsible for safeguarding machines and should consider this need when purchasing machinery. New machinery is usually available with safeguards installed by the manufacturer. You can also purchase appropriate safeguards separately or build them in-house.

Are certain jobs particularly hazardous for some employees?

Yes. Under the *Fair Labor Standards Act*, the Secretary of Labor has designated certain non-farm jobs as especially hazardous for employees under the age of 18. These workers generally are prohibited from operating band saws, circular saws, guillotine shears, punching and shearing machines, meatpacking or meat-processing machines, paper products machines, woodworking machines, metal-forming machines, and meat slicers.

How can I get more information?

You can find more information about amputations, including the full text of OSHA's standards, on OSHA's website at **www.osha.gov**. In addition, publications explaining the subject of amputations in greater detail are available from OSHA. *Concepts and Techniques of Machine Safeguarding* (OSHA 3067) and *Control of Hazardous Energy (Lockout/Tagout)* (OSHA 3120) are available on OSHA's website. For other information about machine guarding see http://www.osha-slc.gov/SLTC/machineguarding/index.html.

A Guide for Protecting Workers from Woodworking Hazards (OSHA 3157) is available either on OSHA's website at **www.osha.gov** or from the Superintendent of Documents, P.O. Box 371954, Pittsburgh, PA 15250-7954, or phone (202) 512-1800, or online at http://bookstore.gpo.gov/index.html.

To file a complaint by phone, report an emergency, or get OSHA advice, assistance, or products, contact your nearest OSHA office under the "U.S. Department of Labor" listing in your phone book, or call us toll-free at **(800) 321-OSHA (6742)**; teletypewriter (TTY) number is (877) 889-5627. To file a complaint online or obtain more information on OSHA federal and state programs, visit OSHA's website at **www.osha.gov**.

This is one in a series of informational fact sheets highlighting OSHA programs, policies, or standards. It does not impose any new compliance requirements or carry the force of legal opinion. For compliance requirements of OSHA standards or regulations, refer to *Title 29 of the Code of Federal Regulations*. This information will be made available to sensory-impaired individuals upon request. Voice phone: (202) 693-1999. See also OSHA's website at **www.osha.gov**.

U.S. Department of Labor
Occupational Safety and Health Administration
2002

Machine guarding

Knowledge check

1. All machines consist of three fundamental areas, including ___.
    a) Flywheels, connecting rods, and transverse moving parts
    b) Point of operation, power transmission device, and operating controls
    c) Reciprocating parts, rotating parts, and on/off switch
    d) Feed mechanisms, auxiliary machine parts, and nip points

2. Rotating, in-running nip points, reciprocating, and transversing are types of hazardous ___.
    a) motions
    b) actions
    c) guards
    d) devices

3. Cutting, punching, shearing, and bending are types of hazardous ___.
    a) motions
    b) actions
    c) guards
    d) devices

4. Which of the following explains how a guard protects workers?
    a) Stops the machine when a worker enters the danger area
    b) Restrains the worker from entering the danger area
    c) Creates distance to keep the worker from entering the danger area
    d) Provides a barrier to prevent access to the danger area

5. Which of the following is an example of a safeguarding device?

    a) Protective shield

    b) Hand-feeding tool

    c) Safety trip control

    d) Awareness barrier

Lockout and tagout

Requirements of the Standard

What are OSHA's requirements?

OSHA's standard establishes minimum performance requirements for controlling hazardous energy. The standard specifies that employers must establish an energy-control program to ensure that employees isolate machines from their energy sources and render them inoperative before any employee services or maintains them.

As part of an energy-control program, employers must:

- Establish energy-control procedures for removing the energy supply from machines and for putting appropriate lockout or tagout devices on the energy-isolating devices to prevent unexpected reenergization. When appropriate, the procedure also must address stored or potentially reaccumulated energy;

- Train employees on the energy-control program, including the safe application, use, and removal of energy controls; and

- Inspect these procedures periodically (at least annually) to ensure that they are being followed and that they remain effective in preventing employee exposure to hazardous energy.

If employers use tagout devices on machinery that can be locked out, they must adopt additional measures to provide the same level of employee protection that lockout devices would provide. Within the broad boundaries of the standard, employers have the flexibility to develop programs and procedures that meet the needs of their individual workplaces and the particular types of machines being maintained or serviced.

What must an energy-control procedure include?

Employers must develop, document, and use procedures to control potentially hazardous energy.[3] The procedures explain what employees must know and do to control hazardous energy effectively when they service or maintain machinery. If this information is the same for the various machines used at a workplace, then a single energy-control procedure may suffice. For example, similar machines (those using the same type and magnitude of energy) that have the same or similar types of control measures can be covered by a single procedure. Employers must develop separate energy-control procedures if their workplaces have more variable conditions such as multiple energy sources, different power connections, or different control sequences that workers must follow to shut down various pieces of machinery.

The energy-control procedures must outline the scope, purpose, authorization, rules, and techniques that employees will use to control hazardous energy sources, as well as the means that will be used to enforce compliance. These procedures must provide employees at least the following information:

- A statement on how to use the procedures;

- Specific procedural steps to shut down, isolate, block, and secure machines;

- Specific steps designating the safe placement, removal, and transfer of lockout/tagout devices and identifying who has responsibility for the lockout/tagout devices; and

- Specific requirements for testing machines to determine and verify the effectiveness of lockout devices, tagout devices, and other energy-control measures.

---

[3] The standard provides a limited exception to the requirement that energy control procedures be documented. If an employer can demonstrate the existence of EACH of the eight elements listed in 1910.147(c)(4)(i), the employer is not required to document the energy control procedure. However, the exception terminates if circumstances change and ANY of the elements no longer exist.

In Appendix A to 1910.147, OSHA provides a *Typical Minimal Lockout Procedure* for employers to consult when preparing their own specific energy-control procedures. The outline is a nonmandatory guideline to help employers and employees comply with the standard. Nothing in the appendix adds to or detracts from any of the requirements in the standard.

What must workers do before they begin service or maintenance activities?

Before beginning service or maintenance, the following steps must be accomplished in sequence and according to the specific provisions of the employer's energy-control procedure:

(1) Prepare for shutdown;

(2) Shut down the machine;

(3) Disconnect or isolate the machine from the energy source(s);

(4) Apply the lockout or tagout device(s) to the energy-isolating device(s);

(5) Release, restrain, or otherwise render safe all potential hazardous stored or residual energy. If a possibility exists for reaccumulation of hazardous energy, regularly verify during the service and maintenance that such energy has not reaccumulated to hazardous levels; and

(6) Verify the isolation and deenergization of the machine.

What must workers do before they remove their lockout or tagout device and reenergize the machine?

Employees who work on deenergized machinery may be seriously injured or killed if someone removes lockout/tagout devices and reenergizes machinery without their knowledge. Thus, it is extremely important that all employees respect lockout and tagout devices and that only the person(s) who applied these devices remove them.

Before removing lockout or tagout devices, the employees must take the following steps in accordance with the specific provisions of the employer's energy-control procedure:

- Inspect machines or their components to assure that they are operationally intact and that nonessential items are removed from the area; and

- Check to assure that everyone is positioned safely and away from machines.

After removing the lockout or tagout devices but before reenergizing the machine, the employer must assure that all employees who operate or work with the machine, as well as those in the area where service or maintenance is performed, know that the devices have been removed and that the machine is capable of being reenergized. (See Sections 6(e) and (f) of 29 CFR Part 1910.147 for specific requirements.) In the rare situation in which the employee who placed the lockout/tagout device is unable to remove that device, another person may remove it under the direction of the employer, provided that the employer strictly adheres to the specific procedures outlined in the standard. (See *29 CFR* 1910.147(e)(3).).

When do I use lockout and how do I do it?

You must use a lockout program (or tagout program that provides a level of protection equal to that achieved through lockout) whenever your employees engage in service or maintenance operations on machines that are capable of being locked out and that expose them to hazardous energy from unexpected energization, startup, or release of stored energy.

The primary way to prevent the release of hazardous energy during service and maintenance activities is by using energy-isolating devices such as manually operated circuit breakers, disconnect switches, and line valves and safety blocks. Lockout requires use of a lock or other lockout device to hold the energy-isolating device in a safe position to prevent machinery from becoming reenergized. Lockout also requires employees to follow an established procedure to ensure that machinery will not be reenergized until the same employee who placed the lockout device on the energy-isolating device removes it.

How can I determine if the energy-isolating device can be locked out?

An energy-isolating device is considered "capable of being locked out" if it meets one of the following requirements:

- Is designed with a hasp or other part to which you can attach a lock such as a lockable electric disconnect switch;

- Has a locking mechanism built into it; or

- Can be locked without dismantling, rebuilding, or replacing the energy-isolating device or permanently altering its energy-control capability, such as a lockable valve cover or circuit breaker blockout.

What do I do if I cannot lock out the equipment?

Sometimes it is not possible to lock out the energy-isolating device associated with the machinery. In that case, you must securely fasten a tagout device as close as safely possible to the energy-isolating device in a position where it will be immediately obvious to anyone attempting to operate the device. You also must meet all of the tagout provisions of the standard. The tag alerts employees to the hazard of reenergization and states that employees may not operate the machinery to which it is attached until the tag is removed in accordance with an established procedure.

What other options do I have?

If it is possible to lock out an energy-isolating device, employers must use lockout devices unless they develop, document, and use a tagout procedure that provides employees with a level of protection equal to that provided by a lockout device. In a tagout program, an employer can attain an equal level of protection by complying with all tagout-related provisions of the standard and using at least one added safety measure that prevents unexpected reenergization. Such measures might include removing an isolating circuit element, blocking a controlling switch, opening an extra disconnecting device, or removing a valve handle to minimize the possibility that machines might inadvertently be reenergized while employees perform service and maintenance activities.

When can tagout devices be used instead of lockout devices?

When an energy-isolating device cannot be locked out, the employer must modify or replace the energy-isolating device to make it capable of being locked out or use a tagout system. Whenever employers significantly repair, renovate, or modify machinery or install new or replacement machinery, however, they must ensure that the energy-isolating devices for the machinery are capable of being locked out.

Tagout devices may be used on energy-isolating devices that are capable of being locked out if the employer develops and implements the tagout in a way that provides employees with a level of protection equal to that achieved through a lockout system.

When using a tagout system, the employer must comply with all tagout-related provisions of the standard and train employees in the limitations of tags, in addition to providing normal hazardous energy control training for all employees.

What are the limitations of tagout devices?

A tagout device is a prominent warning that clearly states that the machinery being controlled must not be operated until the tag is removed in accordance with an established procedure. Tags are essentially warning devices and do not provide the physical restraint of a lock. Tags may evoke a false sense of security. For these reasons, OSHA considers lockout devices to be more secure and more effective than tagout devices in protecting employees from hazardous energy.

What are the requirements for lockout/tagout devices?

Whether lockout or tagout devices are used, they must be the only devices the employer uses in conjunction with energy-isolating devices to control hazardous energy. The employer must provide these devices and they must be singularly identified and not used for other purposes. In addition, they must have the following characteristics:

- Durable enough to withstand workplace conditions. Tagout devices must not deteriorate or become illegible even when used with corrosive components such as acid or alkali chemicals or in wet environments.

- Standardized according to color, shape, or size. Tagout devices also must be standardized according to print and format. Tags must be legible and understandable by all employees. They must warn employees about the hazards if the machine is energized, and offer employees clear instruction such as: "Do Not Start," "Do Not Open," "Do Not Close," "Do Not Energize," or "Do Not Operate."

- Substantial enough to minimize the likelihood of premature or accidental removal. Employees should be able to remove locks only by using excessive force with special tools such as bolt cutters or other metal-cutting tools. Tag attachments must be non-reusable, self-locking, and non-releasable, with a minimum unlocking strength of 50 pounds. Tags must be attachable by hand, and the device for attaching the tag should be a one-piece nylon cable tie or its equivalent so it can withstand all environments and conditions.

- Labeled to identify the specific employees authorized to apply and remove them.

What do employees need to know about lockout/tagout programs?

Training must ensure that employees understand the purpose, function, and restrictions of the energy-control program. Employers must provide training specific to the needs of "authorized," "affected," and "other" employees.

"Authorized" employees are those responsible for implementing the energy-control procedures or performing the service or maintenance activities. They need the knowledge and skills necessary for the safe application, use, and removal of energy-isolating devices. They also need training in the following:

- Hazardous energy source recognition;

- The type and magnitude of the hazardous energy sources in the workplace; and

- Energy-control procedures, including the methods and means to isolate and control those energy sources.

"Affected" employees (usually machine operators or users) are employees who operate the relevant machinery or whose jobs require them to be in the area where service or maintenance is performed. These employees do not service or maintain machinery or perform lockout/tagout activities. Affected employees must receive training in the purpose and use of energy-control procedures. They also need to be able to do the following:

- Recognize when the energy-control procedure is being used,

- Understand the purpose of the procedure, and
- Understand the importance of not tampering with lockout or tagout devices and not starting or using equipment that has been locked or tagged out.

All other employees whose work operations are or may be in an area where energy-control procedures are used must receive instruction regarding the energy-control procedure and the prohibition against removing a lockout or tagout device and attempting to restart, reenergize, or operate the machinery.

In addition, if tagout devices are used, all employees must receive training regarding the limitations of tags. (See *29 CFR* 1910.147(c)(7)(ii).)

When is training necessary?

The employer must provide initial training before starting service and maintenance activities and must provide retraining as necessary. In addition, the employer must certify that the training has been given to all employees covered by the standard. The certification must contain each employee's name and dates of training.

Employers must provide retraining for all authorized and affected employees whenever there is a change in the following:

- Job assignments,
- Machinery or processes that present a new hazard, or
- Energy-control procedures.

Retraining also is necessary whenever a periodic inspection reveals, or an employer has reason to believe, that shortcomings exist in an employee's knowledge or use of the energy-control procedure.

What if I need power to test or position machines, equipment, or components?

OSHA allows the temporary removal of lockout or tagout devices and the reenergization of the machine only in limited situations for particular tasks that require energization—for example, when power is needed to test or position machines, equipment, or components. However, this temporary exception applies only for the limited time required to perform the particular task requiring energization. Employers must provide effective protection from hazardous energy when employees perform these operations. The following steps must be performed in sequence before reenergization:

1. Clear tools and materials from machines.
2. Clear employees from the area around the machines.
3. Remove the lockout or tagout devices as specified in the standard.
4. Energize the machine and proceed with testing or positioning.
5. Deenergize all systems, isolate the machine from the energy source, and reapply energy-control measures if additional service or maintenance is required.

The employer must develop, document, and use energy-control procedures that establish a sequence of actions to follow whenever reenergization is required as a part of a service or maintenance activity, since employees may be exposed to significant risks during these transition periods.

How often do I need to review my lockout/tagout procedures?

Employees are required to review their procedures at least once a year to ensure that they provide adequate worker protection. As part of the review, employers must correct any deviations and inadequacies identified in the energy-control procedure or its application.

What does a review entail?

The periodic inspection is intended to assure that employees are familiar with their responsibilities under the procedure and continue to implement energy-control procedures properly. The inspector, who must be an authorized person not involved in using the particular control procedure being inspected, must be able to determine the following:

- Employees are following steps in the energy-control procedure;
- Employees involved know their responsibilities under the procedure; and
- The procedure is adequate to provide the necessary protection, and what changes, if any, are needed.

For a lockout procedure, the periodic inspection must include a review of each authorized employee's responsibilities under the energy-control procedure being inspected. Where tagout is used, the inspector's review also extends to affected employees because of the increased importance of their role in avoiding accidental or inadvertent activation of the machinery. In addition, the employer must certify that the designated inspectors perform periodic inspections. The certification must specify the following:

- Machine or equipment on which the energy-control procedure was used,
- Date of the inspection,
- Names of employees included in the inspection, and
- Name of the person who performed the inspection.

What if I use outside contractors for service or maintenance procedures?

If an outside contractor services or maintains machinery, the onsite employer and the contractor must inform each other of their respective lockout or tagout procedures. The onsite employer also must ensure that employees understand and comply with all requirements of the contractor's energy-control program(s).

What if a group performs service or maintenance activities?

When a crew, department, or other group performs service or maintenance, they must use a procedure that provides all employees a level of protection equal to that provided by a personal lockout or tagout device. Each employee in the group must have control over the sources of hazardous energy while he or she is involved in service and maintenance activities covered by the standard. Personal control is achieved when each authorized employee affixes a personal lockout/tagout device to a group lockout mechanism instead of relying on a supervisor or other person to provide protection against hazardous energy. Detailed requirements of individual responsibilities are provided in 29 *CFR* 1910.147(f)(3)(ii)(A) through (D). Appendix C of OSHA Directive STD 1-7.3, 29 *CFR* 1910.147, the Control of Hazardous Energy (Lockout/Tagout)-Inspection Procedures and Interpretive Guidance, (September 11, 1990), provides additional guidance.

What if a shift changes during machine service or maintenance?

Employers must make sure that there is a continuity of lockout or tagout protection. This includes the orderly transfer of lockout or tagout device protection between outgoing and incoming shifts to control hazardous energy. When lockout or tagout devices remain on energy-isolation devices from a previous shift, the incoming shift members must verify for themselves that the machinery is effectively isolated and deenergized.

103

Additionally, OSHA offers a variety of web-based tools to help educate employers and employees about the lockout/tagout standard and how to apply it in their workplace. These include the following:

- The Lockout/Tagout Interactive Training Program, which includes a tutorial, five abstracts with a detailed discussion of major lockout/tagout issues involved, and interactive case studies;

- The Lockout/Tagout Plus Expert Advisor, an interactive, expert, diagnostic software package to help users understand and apply OSHA standards that protect workers from the release of hazardous energy; and

- The Lockout/Tagout electronic Compliance Assistant Tool (eCAT), an illustrated tool to help businesses identify and correct workplace hazards.

These tools are available on the OSHA website at www.osha.gov. For the Lockout/Tagout Interactive Training Program, click on **Technical Links**. For the Expert Advisor and eCAT, click on **eTools**.

What additional information does OSHA provide about lockout/tagout?

To gain a more comprehensive understanding of the requirements for controlling hazardous energy, employers and other interested persons should review the following:

- OSHA standards with provisions regarding the control of hazardous energy such as 29 *CFR* 1910.147, The control of hazardous energy (lockout/tagout); 29 *CFR* 1910.269, Electric power generation, transmission, and distribution; and 29 *CFR* 1910.333, Selection and use of work practices. Employers in the maritime, agriculture, and construction industries are urged to review the provisions for the control of hazardous energy contained in 29 *CFR* Parts 1915, 1917, 1918, 1925, and 1926.

- The regulatory preambles to 29 *CFR* 1910.147 (54 *Federal Register* 36644 (September 1, 1989)) and 1910.269 (59 *Federal Register* 4320 (January 31, 1994)), which contain comments from interested parties and OSHA's explanation for the provisions of the standards.

- OSHA instructions concerning the control of hazardous energy—Directive CPL 2-1.18A, Enforcement of the Electrical Power Generation, Transmission, and Distribution Standard (October 20, 1997) and OSHA Directive STD 1-7.3, 29 *CFR* 1910.147, the Control of Hazardous Energy (Lockout/Tagout)-Inspection Procedures and Interpretive Guidance, (September 11, 1990).

- OSHA letters of interpretation regarding the application of standards concerning the control of hazardous energy.

Most of these documents are available on the OSHA website at www.osha.gov.

Permit-required confined spaces

Introduction

Many workplaces contain spaces that are considered to be "confined" because their configurations hinder the activities of employees who must enter into, work in or exit from them. In many instances, employees who work in confined spaces also face increased risk of exposure to serious physical injury from hazards such as entrapment, engulfment and hazardous atmospheric conditions. Confinement itself may pose entrapment hazards and work in confined spaces may keep employees closer to hazards such as machinery components than they would be otherwise. For example, confinement, limited access and restricted airflow can result in hazardous conditions that would not normally arise in an open workplace.

The terms "permit-required confined space" and "permit space" refer to spaces that meet OSHA's definition of a "confined space" and contain health or safety hazards. For this reason, OSHA requires workers to have a permit to enter these spaces. Throughout this publication, the term "permit space" will be used to describe a "permit-required confined space."

Definitions

By definition, a **confined space**:

- Is large enough for an employee to enter fully and perform assigned work;
- Is not designed for continuous occupancy by the employee; and
- Has a limited or restricted means of entry or exit.

These spaces may include underground vaults, tanks, storage bins, pits and diked areas, vessels, silos and other similar areas.

By definition, a **permit-required confined space** has one or more of these characteristics:

- Contains or has the potential to contain a hazardous atmosphere;
- Contains a material with the potential to engulf someone who enters the space;
- Has an internal configuration that might cause an entrant to be trapped or asphyxiated by inwardly converging walls or by a floor that slopes downward and tapers to a smaller cross section; and/or
- Contains any other recognized serious safety or health hazards.

OSHA's Confined Space Standard

OSHA's standard for confined spaces (29 CFR 1910.146) contains the requirements for practices and procedures to protect employ-ees in general industry from the hazards of entering permit spaces.

Employers in general industry must evaluate their workplaces to determine if spaces are permit spaces. (See flow chart, page 5.) If a workplace contains permit spaces, the employer must inform exposed employees of their existence, location and the hazards they pose. This can be done by posting danger signs such as "DANGER—PERMIT-REQUIRED CONFINED SPACE—AUTHORIZED ENTRANTS ONLY" or using an equally effective means.

If employees are not to enter and work in permit spaces, employers must take effective measures to prevent them from entering these spaces. If employees are expected to enter permit spaces, the employer must develop a written permit space program and make it available to employees or their representatives.

Alternative to a full permit entry

Under certain conditions described in the standard, the employer may use alternate procedures for worker entry into a permit space. For example, if an employer can demonstrate with monitoring and inspection data that the only hazard is an actual or potential hazardous atmosphere that can be made safe for entry using continuous forced air ventilation, the employer may be exempted from some requirements, such as permits and attendants. However, even in these circumstances, the employer must test the internal atmosphere of the space for oxygen content, flammable gases and vapors, and the potential for toxic air contaminants before any employee enters it. The employer must also provide continuous ventilation and verify that the required measurements are performed before entry.

Written Programs

Any employer who allows employee entry into a permit space must develop and implement a written program for the space. Among other things, the OSHA standard requires the employer's written program to:

- Implement necessary measures to prevent unauthorized entry;
- Identify and evaluate permit space hazards before allowing employee entry;
- Test atmospheric conditions in the permit space before entry operations and monitor the space during entry;
- Perform appropriate testing for the following atmospheric hazards in this sequence: oxygen, combustible gases or vapors, and toxic gases or vapors;
- Establish and implement the means, procedures and practices to eliminate or control hazards necessary for safe permit space entry operations;
- Identify employee job duties;
- Provide and maintain, at no cost to the employee, personal protective equipment and any other equipment necessary for safe entry and require employees to use it;
- Ensure that at least one attendant is stationed outside the permit space for the duration of entry operations;
- Coordinate entry operations when employees of more than one employer are working in the permit space;
- Implement appropriate procedures for summoning rescue and emergency services, and preventing unauthorized personnel from attempting rescue;
- Establish, in writing, and implement a system for the preparation, issue, use and cancellation of entry permits;
- Review established entry operations annually and revise the permit space entry program as necessary; and
- Implement the procedures that any attendant who is required to monitor multiple spaces will follow during an emergency in one or more of those spaces.

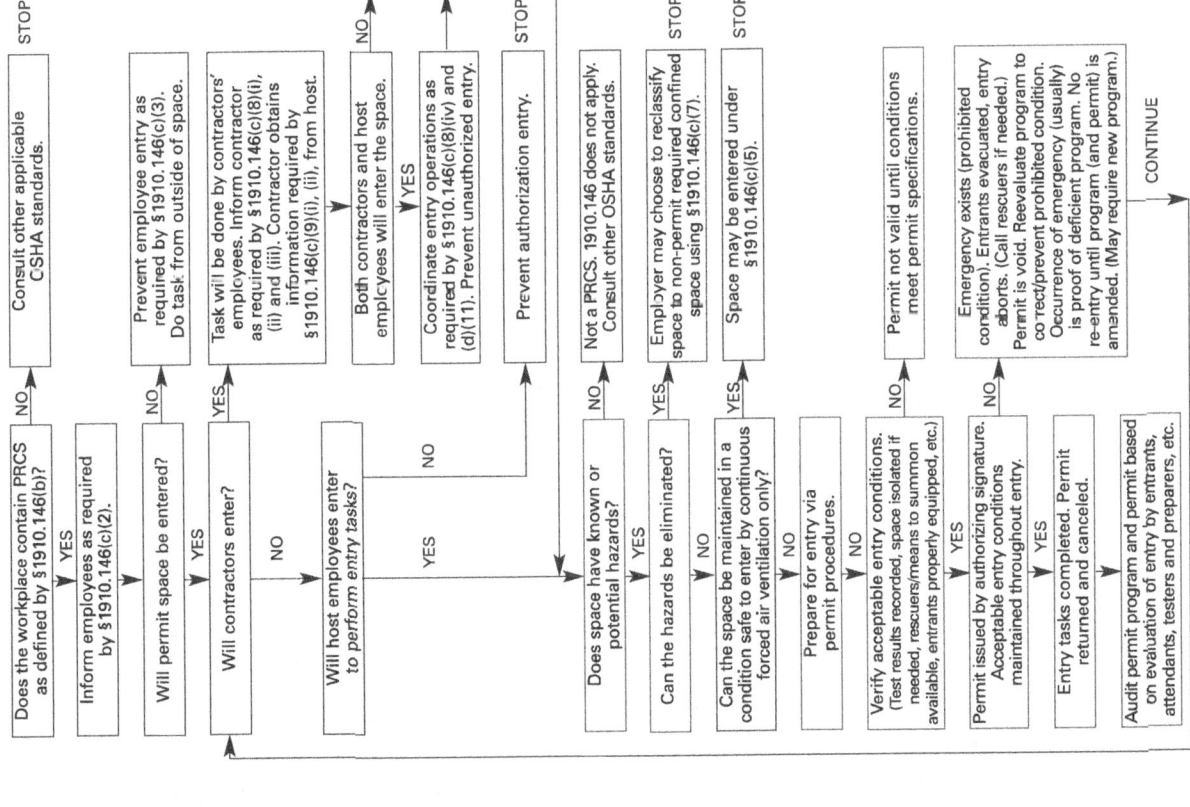

Permit-Required Confined Space Decision Flow Chart

[1] Spaces may have to be evacuated and reevaluated if hazards arise during entry.

Source: 29 CFR 1910.146 Appendix A.

Informing Contract Employees

Employers must inform any contractors whom they hire to enter permit spaces about:

- The permit spaces and permit space entry requirements;
- Any identified hazards;
- The employer's experience with the space, such as knowledge of hazardous conditions; and
- Precautions or procedures to be followed when in or near permit spaces.

When employees of more than one employer are conducting entry operations, the affected employers must coordinate entry operations to ensure that affected employees are appropriately protected from permit space hazards. The employer also must give contractors any other pertinent information regarding hazards and operations in permit spaces and be debriefed at the conclusion of entry operations.

Entry Permits

A permit, signed by the entry supervisor, must be posted at all entrances or otherwise made available to entrants before they enter a permit space. The permit must verify that pre-entry preparations outlined in the standard have been completed. The duration of entry permits must not exceed the time required to complete an assignment.

Entry permits must include:

- Name of permit space to be entered, authorized entrant(s), eligible attendants and individuals authorized to be entry supervisors;
- Test results;
- Tester's initials or signature;
- Name and signature of supervisor who authorizes entry;
- Purpose of entry and known space hazards;
- Measures to be taken to isolate permit spaces and to eliminate or control space hazards;

Controlling Hazards

The employer's written program should establish the means, procedures and practices to eliminate or control hazards necessary for safe permit space entry operations. These may include:

- Specifying acceptable entry conditions;
- Isolating the permit space;
- Providing barriers;
- Verifying acceptable entry conditions; and
- Purging, making inert, flushing or ventilating the permit space.

Equipment for safe entry

In addition to personal protective equipment, other equipment that employees may require for safe entry into a permit space includes:

- Testing, monitoring, ventilating, communications and lighting equipment;
- Barriers and shields;
- Ladders; and
- Retrieval devices.

Detection of hazardous conditions

If hazardous conditions are detected during entry, employees must immediately leave the space. The employer must evaluate the space to determine the cause of the hazardous atmosphere and modify the program as necessary.

When entry to permit spaces is prohibited, the employer must take effective measures to prevent unauthorized entry. Non-permit confined spaces must be evaluated when changes occur in their use or configuration and, where appropriate, must be reclassified as permit spaces.

A space with no potential to have atmospheric hazards may be classified as a non-permit confined space only when all hazards are eliminated in accordance with the standard. If entry is required to eliminate hazards and obtain data, the employer must follow specific procedures in the standard.

and their authorized representatives. The record must include the employee's name, the trainer's signature or initials and dates of the training.

Assigned Duties

Authorized entrant

Authorized entrants are required to:

- Know space hazards, including information on the means of exposure such as inhalation or dermal absorption, signs of symptoms and consequences of the exposure;
- Use appropriate personal protective equipment properly;
- Maintain communication with attendants as necessary to enable them to monitor the entrant's status and alert the entrant to evacuate when necessary;
- Exit from the permit space as soon as possible when:
  - Ordered by the authorized person;
  - He or she recognizes the warning signs or symptoms of exposure;
  - A prohibited condition exists; or
  - An automatic alarm is activated.
- Alert the attendant when a prohibited condition exists or when warning signs or symptoms of exposure exist.

Attendant

The attendant is required to:

- Remain outside the permit space during entry operations unless relieved by another authorized attendant;
- Perform non-entry rescues when specified by the employer's rescue procedure;
- Know existing and potential hazards, including information on the mode of exposure, signs or symptoms, consequences and physiological effects;
- Name and telephone numbers of rescue and emergency services and means to be used to contact them;
- Date and authorized duration of entry;
- Acceptable entry conditions;
- Communication procedures and equipment to maintain contact during entry;
- Additional permits, such as for hot work, that have been issued authorizing work in the permit space;
- Special equipment and procedures, including personal protective equipment and alarm systems; and
- Any other information needed to ensure employee safety.

Cancelled entry permits

The entry supervisor must cancel entry permits when an assignment is completed or when new conditions exist. New conditions must be noted on the cancelled permit and used in revising the permit space program. The standard requires that the employer keep all canceled entry permits for at least one year.

Worker Training

Before the initial work assignment begins, the employer must provide proper training for all workers who are required to work in permit spaces. After the training, employers must ensure that the employees have acquired the understanding, knowledge and skills necessary to safely perform their duties. Additional training is required when:

- The job duties change;
- A change occurs in the permit space program or the permit space operation presents any new hazard; and
- An employee's job performance shows deficiencies.

In addition to this training, rescue team members also require training in CPR and first aid. Employers must certify that this training has been provided.

After completion of training, the employer must keep a record of employee training and make it available for inspection by employees

- Maintain communication with and keep an accurate account of those workers entering the permit space;
- Order evacuation of the permit space when:
  - A prohibited condition exists;
  - A worker shows signs of physiological effects of hazard exposure;
  - An emergency outside the confined space exists; and
  - The attendant cannot effectively and safely perform required duties.
- Summon rescue and other services during an emergency;
- Ensure that unauthorized people stay away from permit spaces or exit immediately if they have entered the permit space;
- Inform authorized entrants and the entry supervisor if any unauthorized person enters the permit space; and
- Perform no other duties that interfere with the attendant's primary duties.

Entry supervisor

Entry supervisors are required to:

- Know space hazards including information on the mode of exposure, signs or symptoms and consequences;
- Verify emergency plans and specified entry conditions such as permits, tests, procedures and equipment before allowing entry;
- Terminate entry and cancel permits when entry operations are completed or if a new condition exists;
- Verify that rescue services are available and that the means for summoning them are operable;
- Take appropriate measures to remove unauthorized entrants; and
- Ensure that entry operations remain consistent with the entry permit and that acceptable entry conditions are maintained.

Emergencies

Rescue service personnel

The standard requires employers to ensure that responders are capable of responding to an emergency in a timely manner. Employers must provide rescue service personnel with personal protective and rescue equipment, including respirators, and training in how to use it. Rescue service personnel also must receive the authorized entrants training and be trained to perform assigned rescue duties.

The standard also requires that all rescuers be trained in first aid and CPR. At a minimum, one rescue team member must be currently certified in first aid and CPR. Employers must ensure that practice rescue exercises are performed yearly and that rescue services are provided access to permit spaces so they can practice rescue operations. Rescuers also must be informed of the hazards of the permit space.

Harnesses and retrieval lines

Authorized entrants who enter a permit space must wear a chest or full body harness with a retrieval line attached to the center of their backs near shoulder level or above their heads. Wristlets may be used if the employer can demonstrate that the use of a chest or full body harness is not feasible or creates a greater hazard.

Also, the employer must ensure that the other end of the retrieval line is attached to a mechanical device or a fixed point outside the permit space. A mechanical device must be available to retrieve someone from vertical type permit spaces more than five feet (1.524 meters) deep.

MSDS

If an injured entrant is exposed to a substance for which a Material Safety Data Sheet (MSDS) or other similar written information is required to be kept at the worksite, that MSDS or other written information must be made available to the medical facility personnel treating the exposed entrant.

Introduction to Ergonomics

FACTSHEET A 1

What Are Musculoskeletal Disorders?

Our bodies normally recover from the wear and tear of work after a period of rest. But if the stresses continue day after day without time to recover, the damage can lead to ergonomic injuries.

Many different terms are used to describe these ergonomic injuries. For example:

- **Cumulative trauma disorders (CTDs).** Ergonomic injuries involve strain that may develop, or accumulate, over time.

- **Repetitive strain injuries (RSIs).** Ergonomic injuries are often caused by repeating the same motions over and over.

- **Musculoskeletal disorders (MSDs).** Ergonomic injuries affect the muscles, bones, tendons, nerves, and tissues.

These terms do not necessarily refer to different conditions. Many ergonomic injuries can be described in all three ways.

These disorders include a number of specific diseases such as carpal tunnel syndrome, bursitis, and tendinitis. Back injuries are the most common and most costly MSD.

Symptoms of these disorders are most common in the back, hands, arms, wrists, elbows, neck, and shoulders. They include:

- Soreness or pain (aching or sharp)
- Stiffness
- Swelling
- Loss of coordination
- Numbness
- Tingling (as though the area is "asleep")
- Unexplained weakness

2 FACTSHEET A — WHAT ARE MUSCULOSKELETAL DISORDERS?

If your work exposes you to any of the ergonomic risk factors described in Factsheet B, these symptoms may be signs that you have an MSD.

It is important to seek medical care if these symptoms:

- Last for more than a week
- Bother you so much that you restrict activities or take time off to recover.

If You Believe You Have an MSD

- Seek early treatment. The longer you have symptoms without getting help, the harder they can be to treat successfully.

- Find a doctor who understands work-related health problems. Don't be afraid to educate your doctor about the possible causes of MSDs at your workplace.

- If your problem is work-related, file a workers' compensation claim to cover lost work time and/or medical costs.

- Don't return to the same working conditions that caused your problem. Work with others at your workplace to ensure that the equipment or activities that contributed to your injury are changed.

- Above all, don't let your condition get you down. Finding the right doctor, getting effective treatment, and improving your work environment take persistence and energy. Don't hesitate to ask for help and don't give up until the problem is solved.

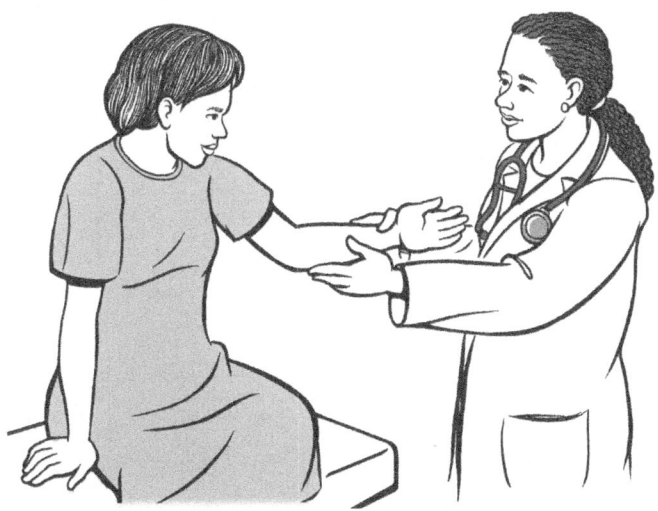

113

FACTSHEET B 1

Risk Factors for Ergonomic Injuries

The field of ergonomics examines the fit between workers and their jobs. It looks at:

- What body movements and positions people use when they work.
- What tools and equipment they use.
- The physical environment (temperature, noise, lighting, etc.).
- The organizational environment (deadlines, teamwork, supervision).
- Whether any of these factors may place a worker at risk of injuries or illnesses.

The goal of ergonomics is to fit workplace conditions and job demands to the capabilities of the individual worker, instead of making the worker fit the job.

To prevent injuries, *ergonomic risk factors* must be identified. Ergonomic risk factors are workplace situations that cause wear and tear on the body and can cause injury. Once these have been identified, you can work on finding ways to eliminate them.

Ergonomic Risk Factors

RISK FACTORS	DEFINITION	POSSIBLE SOLUTIONS
Repetition	Making the same motion over and over.	Redesign task to reduce repetitions; increase rest time between repetitions; rotate among tasks with different motions.
Awkward Posture	Prolonged bending, reaching, kneeling, squatting, or twisting any part of your body.	Redesign tasks and equipment to keep the body in more "neutral" positions.
Forceful Motion	Excessive effort needed to do tasks such as pulling, pounding, pushing, and lifting.	Redesign task to reduce the exertion needed; assign more staff; use mechanical assists.
Stationary Position	Staying in one position too long, causing fatigue in muscles and joints.	Redesign task to avoid stationary positions; provide opportunities to change position.
Direct Pressure	Prolonged contact of the body with a hard surface or edge.	Improve tool and equipment design or layout to eliminate pressure; provide cushioning material.
Vibration	Using vibrating tools or equipment.	Insulate the hand or body from vibration; keep tools or equipment in good condition to reduce excessive vibration.
Extreme Temperature	Working where it is too hot or too cold. Cold reduces feeling, blood flow, and strength. Heat increases fatigue.	Control temperature where possible; insulate the body against cold by wearing gloves and warm clothing; provide breaks and fresh water in hot environments.
Work Stress	Includes machine-paced work, inadequate breaks, monotonous tasks, multiple deadlines, poor work organization, or poor supervision.	Establish reasonable workload, sufficient breaks, task variety, individual autonomy.

- The more risk factors you face, the greater your chance of injury.
- The longer you are exposed to a risk factor, the greater your chance of injury.
- By reducing or eliminating risk factors, the chance of injury can be decreased.

Identifying Risk Factors

Below are some ways to identify ergonomic risk factors.

TALK TO WORKERS: SURVEYS OR INTERVIEWS

Workers are often the best source of information on the potential problems posed by their jobs. You can conduct a written survey or talk to people individually. Factsheet C is a sample worker health survey.

LOOK AT JOBS: INSPECTIONS AND JOB EVALUATIONS

Conduct a walkaround inspection of the workplace to see which jobs or tasks may pose ergonomic problems. Those jobs can then be evaluated to identify specific risk factors. When evaluating a job, break the work down into the smallest pieces possible so that you can be specific and detailed.

Once you have watched people do their work and asked them about it, use a checklist or similar form to record risk factors as well as to track your progress in resolving a problem. Factsheet D is a sample ergonomics inspection checklist.

Below are some tips for conducting job evaluations.

A job evaluation should include three parts:

- **Discussion.** Talk to the people doing the job. Ask whether they experience pain or discomfort while performing the job and what specific activities seem to trigger that pain. Understanding the relationship between pain and specific activities can help you pinpoint tasks, workstations, equipment, or tools which may be causing or aggravating injuries.

- **Job description.** Collect information that fully describes each specific task, job, workstation, tool, and/or piece of equipment that you evaluate. Include information about speed, production requirements, and work schedule, including break times. See if there is a written job description available and supplement it with your own notes.

- **Observation and measurement.** Use direct observation, videotapes, photos, and sketches to identify risk factors. Use a checklist to record specific risk factors, including the weights of objects, how long they are held, or how far they are moved.

Introduction to Ergonomics

Knowledge check

1. Ergonomics is the science of ____.

    a) designing the job to fit the worker

    b) fitting the worker to the job

    c) lifting injuries

    d) safety and health

2. MSDs account for approximately ____ of all injuries and illnesses.

    a) 1%

    b) 10%

    c) 33%

    d) 54%

3. Which of the following is an example of an ergonomic risk factor?

    a) Neutral postures

    b) Rest

    c) Repetition

    d) Personal protective equipment

4. Ergonomic hazards can be prevented or reduced by which of the following control methods?

    a) Engineering controls

    b) Proper work practices/administrative controls

    c) Personal protective equipment

    d) All of the above

Bloodborne pathogens

OSHA FactSheet

OSHA's Bloodborne Pathogens Standard

Bloodborne pathogens are infectious microorganisms present in blood that can cause disease in humans. These pathogens include, but are not limited to, hepatitis B virus (HBV), hepatitis C virus (HCV), and human immunodeficiency virus (HIV), the virus that causes AIDS. Workers exposed to bloodborne pathogens are at risk for serious or life-threatening illnesses.

Protections Provided by OSHA's Bloodborne Pathogens Standard

All of the requirements of OSHA's Bloodborne Pathogens standard can be found in Title 29 of the Code of Federal Regulations at 29 CFR 1910.1030. The standard's requirements state what employers must do to protect workers who are occupationally exposed to blood or other potentially infectious materials (OPIM), as defined in the standard. That is, the standard protects workers who can reasonably be anticipated to come into contact with blood or OPIM as a result of doing their job duties.

In general, the standard requires employers to:

- **Establish an exposure control plan.** This is a written plan to eliminate or minimize occupational exposures. The employer must prepare an exposure determination that contains a list of job classifications in which all workers have occupational exposure and a list of job classifications in which some workers have occupational exposure, along with a list of the tasks and procedures performed by those workers that result in their exposure.

- **Employers must update the plan annually** to reflect changes in tasks, procedures, and positions that affect occupational exposure, and also technological changes that eliminate or reduce occupational exposure. In addition, employers must annually document in the plan that they have considered and begun using appropriate, commercially-available effective safer medical devices designed to eliminate or minimize occupational exposure. Employers must also document that they have solicited input from frontline workers in identifying, evaluating, and selecting effective engineering and work practice controls.

- **Implement the use of universal precautions** (treating all human blood and OPIM as if known to be infectious for bloodborne pathogens).

- **Identify and use engineering controls.** These are devices that isolate or remove the bloodborne pathogens hazard from the workplace. They include sharps disposal containers, self-sheathing needles, and safer medical devices, such as sharps with engineered sharps-injury protection and needleless systems.

- **Identify and ensure the use of work practice controls.** These are practices that reduce the possibility of exposure by changing the way a task is performed, such as appropriate practices for handling and disposing of contaminated sharps, handling specimens, handling laundry, and cleaning contaminated surfaces and items.

- **Provide personal protective equipment (PPE), such as gloves, gowns, eye protection, and masks.** Employers must clean, repair, and replace this equipment as needed. Provision, maintenance, repair and replacement are at no cost to the worker.

- **Make available hepatitis B vaccinations to all workers with occupational exposure.** This vaccination must be offered after the worker has received the required bloodborne pathogens training and within 10 days of initial assignment to a job with occupational exposure.

- **Make available post-exposure evaluation and follow-up to any occupationally exposed worker who experiences an exposure incident.** An exposure incident is a specific eye, mouth, other mucous membrane, non-intact skin, or parenteral contact with blood or OPIM. This evaluation and follow-up must be at no cost to the worker and includes documenting the route(s) of exposure and the circumstances under which the exposure incident occurred; identifying and testing the source individual for HBV and HIV infectivity, if the source individual consents or the law does not require consent; collecting and testing the exposed worker's blood, if the worker consents; offering post-exposure prophylaxis; offering counseling; and evaluating reported illnesses. The healthcare professional will provide a limited written opinion to the employer and all diagnoses must remain confidential.

- **Use labels and signs to communicate hazards.** Warning labels must be affixed to containers of regulated waste; containers of contaminated reusable sharps; refrigerators and freezers containing blood or OPIM; other containers used to store, transport, or ship blood or OPIM; contaminated equipment that is being shipped or serviced; and bags or containers of contaminated laundry, except as provided in the standard. Facilities may use red bags or red containers instead of labels. In HIV and HBV research laboratories and production facilities, signs must be posted at all access doors when OPIM or infected animals are present in the work area or containment module.

- **Provide information and training to workers.** Employers must ensure that their workers receive regular training that covers all elements of the standard including, but not limited to: information on bloodborne pathogens and diseases, methods used to control occupational exposure, hepatitis B vaccine, and medical evaluation and post-exposure follow-up procedures. Employers must offer this training on initial assignment, at least annually thereafter, and when new or modified tasks or procedures affect a worker's occupational exposure. Also, HIV and HBV laboratory and production facility workers must receive specialized initial training, in addition to the training provided to all workers with occupational exposure. Workers must have the opportunity to ask the trainer questions. Also, training must be presented at an educational level and in a language that workers understand.

- **Maintain worker medical and training records.** The employer also must maintain a sharps injury log, unless it is exempt under Part 1904 -- Recording and Reporting Occupational Injuries and Illnesses, in Title 29 of the Code of Federal Regulations.

Additional Information

For more information, go to OSHA's Bloodborne Pathogens and Needlestick Prevention Safety and Health Topics web page at: https://www.osha.gov/SLTC/bloodbornepathogens/index.html.

To file a complaint by phone, report an emergency, or get OSHA advice, assistance, or products, contact your nearest OSHA office under the "U.S. Department of Labor" listing in your phone book, or call us toll-free at **(800) 321-OSHA (6742)**.

This is one in a series of informational fact sheets highlighting OSHA programs, policies or standards. It does not impose any new compliance requirements. For a comprehensive list of compliance requirements of OSHA standards or regulations, refer to Title 29 of the Code of Federal Regulations. This information will be made available to sensory-impaired individuals upon request. The voice phone is (202) 693-1999; the teletypewriter (TTY) number is (877) 889-5627.

For assistance, contact us. We can help. It's confidential.

DSG 1/2011

OSHA® FactSheet

Personal Protective Equipment (PPE) Reduces Exposure to Bloodborne Pathogens

OSHA's Bloodborne Pathogens standard (29 CFR 1910.1030) requires employers to protect workers who are occupationally exposed to blood and other potentially infectious materials (OPIM), as defined in the standard. That is, the standard protects workers who can reasonably be anticipated to come into contact with blood or OPIM as a result of doing their job duties.

One way the employer can protect workers against exposure to bloodborne pathogens, such as hepatitis B virus (HBV), hepatitis C virus (HCV), and human immunodeficiency virus (HIV), the virus that causes AIDS, is by providing and ensuring they use personal protective equipment, or PPE. Wearing appropriate PPE can significantly reduce risk, since it acts as a barrier against exposure. Employers are required to provide, clean, repair, and replace this equipment as needed, and at no cost to workers.

Selecting Personal Protective Equipment

Personal protective equipment may include gloves, gowns, laboratory coats, face shields or masks, eye protection, pocket masks, and other protective gear. The PPE selected must be appropriate for the task. This means the level and type of protection must fit the expected exposure. For example, gloves may be the only PPE needed for a laboratory technician who is drawing blood. However, a pathologist conducting an autopsy would need much more protective clothing because of the different types of exposure (e.g., splashes, sprays) and the increased amount of blood and OPIM that are encountered. PPE must be readily accessible to workers and available in appropriate sizes.

If it can be reasonably expected that a worker could have hand contact with blood, OPIM, or contaminated surfaces or items, the employer must ensure that the worker wears gloves. Single-use gloves cannot be washed or decontaminated for reuse. Utility gloves may be decontaminated if their ability to provide an effective barrier is not compromised. They should be replaced when they show signs of cracking, peeling, tearing, puncturing, or deteriorating. Non-latex gloves, glove liners, powderless gloves or similar alternatives must be provided if workers are allergic to the gloves normally provided.

Gloves are required for all phlebotomies outside of volunteer blood donation centers. If an employer in a volunteer blood donation center judges that routine gloving for all phlebotomies is not necessary, then the employer is required to periodically re-evaluate this policy; make gloves available for workers who want to use them; and cannot discourage their use. In addition, employers must ensure that workers in volunteer blood donation centers use gloves (1) when they have cuts, scratches or other breaks in their skin, (2) while they are in training, or (3) when the worker believes that hand contamination might occur.

When splashes, sprays, splatters, or droplets of blood or OPIM pose a hazard to the eyes, nose or mouth, then masks in conjunction with eye protection (such as goggles or glasses with solid side shields) or chin-length face shields must be worn. Protection against exposure to the body is provided by protective clothing, such as gowns, aprons, lab coats, and similar garments. Surgical caps or hoods, and shoe covers or boots are needed when gross contamination is expected, such as during orthopedic surgery or autopsies.

In HIV and HBV research laboratories and production facilities, laboratory coats, gowns, smocks, uniforms, or other appropriate protective clothing must be used in work areas and animal rooms. Also, protective clothing must not be worn outside of the work area and must be decontaminated before being laundered.

Exception to Use of Personal Protective Equipment

A worker may choose, temporarily and briefly, **under rare and extraordinary circumstances**, to forego use of personal protective equipment. It must be the worker's professional judgment that using the personal protective equipment would prevent the delivery of health care or public safety services or would pose an increased hazard to the safety of the worker or coworker. When such a situation occurs, the employer is required to investigate and document the circumstances to determine if there is a way to avoid it from happening again in the future. Employers and workers should be aware that this is not a blanket exemption to the requirement to use PPE. OSHA expects that this will be an extremely rare occurrence.

Decontaminating and Disposing of Personal Protective Equipment

Employers must ensure that workers remove personal protective equipment before leaving the work area. If a garment is penetrated by blood or OPIM, it must be removed immediately or as soon as feasible. Once PPE is removed, it must be placed in an appropriately designated area or container for storage, washing, decontamination, or disposal. In addition, employers must ensure that workers wash their hands immediately or as soon as feasible after removal of gloves or other personal protective equipment.

Additional Information

For more information, go to OSHA's Bloodborne Pathogens and Needlestick Prevention Safety and Health Topics web page at: https://www.osha.gov/SLTC/bloodbornepathogens/index.html.

To file a complaint by phone, report an emergency, or get OSHA advice, assistance, or products, contact your nearest OSHA office under the "U.S. Department of Labor" listing in your phone book, or call us toll-free at (800) 321-OSHA (6742).

This is one in a series of informational fact sheets highlighting OSHA programs, policies or standards. It does not impose any new compliance requirements. For a comprehensive list of compliance requirements of OSHA standards or regulations, refer to Title 29 of the Code of Federal Regulations. This information will be made available to sensory-impaired individuals upon request. The voice phone is (202) 693-1999; teletypewriter (TTY) number: (877) 889-5627.

For assistance, contact us. We can help. It's confidential.

OSHA® Occupational Safety and Health Administration
www.osha.gov   1-800-321-6742

DSG 1/2011

Bloodborne pathogens

Knowledge check

1. Bloodborne pathogens can be transmitted by ____.

    a) sexual intercourse or intravenous drug use

    b) rubbing an eye after coming in contact with potentially infectious material

    c) potentially infectious material coming in contact with inflamed acne or sunburn blisters

    d) all of the above

2. Employees should use PPE when _____.

    a) there is a reasonable anticipation of contact with blood or OPIM

    b) cleaning up spills

    c) responding to an emergency

    d) all of the above

3. Which of the following is an example of a work practice control?

    a) Spill kits

    b) Accessible hand-washing stations

    c) Proper decontamination of spill areas

    d) Red hazardous waste bags

4. Which of the following is a standard precaution for workers exposed to bloodborne pathogens?

    a) Treat all liquids as hazardous for HIV

    b) Treat all blood and bodily fluids of patients as potentially infectious materials

    c) Test all blood and unknown bodily fluids for HIV after spills

    d) Label unknown liquids with hazard signs

5. Hepatitis B is an inflammation of which body organ?

   a) Kidney

   b) Lungs

   c) Larynx

   d) Liver

6. In the event of an exposure incident, which following action should be taken first?

   a) Notify appropriate personnel

   b) Wash the area thoroughly

   c) Seek medical treatment

   d) Complete an incident or accident report

7. Which of the following actions can help prevent exposure to bloodborne pathogens?

   a) Wearing latex gloves

   b) Wearing goggles

   c) Washing hands

   d) All of the above

8. A vaccine is only available for which of the following major bloodborne pathogen viruses?

   a) HIV

   b) Hepatitis B

   c) Hepatitis C

   d) No vaccines are available for any of the three major BBP viruses

9. Which of the following are potential routes of entry for bloodborne pathogens?

   a) Mucous membranes of the eyes, nose, and mouth

   b) Non-intact skin

   c) Penetration by a contaminated sharp object

   d) All of the above

Exit routes, Emergency Action Plans, Fire Prevention Plans, and fire protection

Emergency Exit Routes

How would you escape from your workplace in an emergency? Do you know where all the exits are in case your first choice is too crowded? Are you sure the doors will be unlocked and that the exit access, such as a hallway, will not be blocked during a fire, explosion, or other crisis? Knowing the answers to these questions could keep you safe during an emergency.

What is an *exit route*?

An *exit route* is a continuous and unobstructed path of exit travel from any point within a workplace to a place of safety. An *exit route* consists of three parts:

- *Exit access* – portion of an *exit route* that leads to an exit.
- *Exit* – portion of an exit route that is generally separated from other areas to provide a protected way of travel to the *exit discharge*.
- *Exit discharge* – part of the *exit route* that leads directly outside or to a street, walkway, refuge area, public way, or open space with access to the outside.

How many *exit routes* must a workplace have?

Normally, a workplace must have at least two *exit routes* to permit prompt evacuation of employees and other building occupants during an emergency. More than two exits are required, however, if the number of employees, size of the building, or arrangement of the workplace will not allow employees to evacuate safely. *Exit routes* must be located as far away as practical from each other in case one is blocked by fire or smoke.

Exception: If the number of employees, the size of the building, its occupancy, or the arrangement of the workplace allows all employees to evacuate safely during an emergency, one *exit route* is permitted.

What are some other design and construction requirements for *exit routes*?

- *Exit routes* must be permanent parts of the workplace.
- *Exit discharges* must lead directly outside or to a street, walkway, refuge area, public way, or open space with access to the outside. These *exit discharge* areas must be large enough to accommodate the building occupants likely to use the *exit route*.
- *Exit stairs* that continue beyond the level on which the *exit discharge* is located must be interrupted at that level by doors, partitions, or other effective means that clearly indicate the direction of travel leading to the *exit discharge*.
- *Exit route* doors must be unlocked from the inside. They must be free of devices or alarms that could restrict use of the *exit route* if the device or alarm fails.
- Side-hinged exit doors must be used to connect rooms to *exit routes*. These doors must swing out in the direction of exit travel if the room is to be occupied by more than 50 people or if the room is a high-hazard area.
- *Exit routes* must support the maximum permitted occupant load for each floor served, and the capacity of an *exit route* may not decrease in the direction of *exit route* travel to the *exit discharge*.
- Ceilings of *exit routes* must be at least 7 feet, 6 inches high.
- An exit access must be at least 28 inches wide at all points. Where there is only one exit access leading to an exit or exit discharge, the width of the exit and exit discharge must be at least equal to the width of the exit access. Objects that project into the exit must not reduce its width.
- Outdoor *exit routes* are permitted but must meet the minimum height and width requirement for indoor *exit routes* and must
  - have guardrails to protect unenclosed sides if a fall hazard exists;
  - be covered if snow or ice is likely to accumulate, unless the employer can demonstrate accumulations will be removed before a slipping hazard exists;
  - be reasonably straight and have smooth, solid, substantially level walkways; and
  - not have a dead-end longer than 20 feet.

What are the requirements for exits?

- *Exits* must be separated by fire resistant materials—that is, one-hour fire-resistance rating if the exit connects three or fewer stories and two-hour fire-resistance rating if the exit connects more than three floors.
- *Exits* are permitted to have only those openings necessary to allow access to the *exit* from occupied areas of the workplace or to the *exit discharge*. Openings must be protected by a self-closing, approved *fire door* that remains closed or automatically closes in an emergency.

What are the maintenance, safeguarding, and operational features for *exit routes*?

OSHA standards require employers to do the following:

- Keep *exit routes* free of explosive or highly flammable furnishings and other decorations.
- Arrange *exit routes* so employees will not have to travel toward a high-hazard area unless the path of travel is effectively shielded from the high-hazard area.
- Ensure that *exit routes* are unobstructed such as by materials, equipment, locked doors, or dead-end corridors.
- Ensure that safeguards designed to protect employees during an emergency remain in good working order.
- Provide lighting for *exit routes* adequate for employees with normal vision.
- Keep *exit route* doors free of decorations or signs that obscure the visibility of *exit route* doors.
- Post signs along the *exit access* indicating the direction of travel to the nearest *exit* and *exit discharge* if that direction is not immediately apparent. Also, the line-of-sight to an exit sign must be clearly visible at all times.
- Mark doors or passages along an *exit access* that could be mistaken for an *exit* "Not an Exit" or with a sign identifying its use (such as "Closet").
- Install "EXIT" signs in plainly legible letters.
- Renew fire-retardant paints or solutions often enough to maintain their fire-retardant properties.
- Maintain *exit routes* during construction, repairs, or alterations.
- Provide an emergency alarm system to alert employees, unless employees can promptly see or smell a fire or other hazard in time to provide adequate warning to them.

Are employers required to have emergency action plans?

If you have *10 or fewer employees*, you may communicate your plan orally. If you have *more than 10 employees*, however, your plan must be written, kept in the workplace, and available for employee review. Although employers are required to have an emergency action plan (EAP) only when the applicable OSHA standard requires it, OSHA strongly recommends that all employers have an EAP. Here are the OSHA standards that require EAP's:

- Process Safety Management of Highly Hazardous Chemicals - 1910.119
- Fixed Extinguishing Systems, General - 1910.160
- Fire Detection Systems, 1910.164
- Grain Handling - 1910.272
- Ethylene Oxide - 1910.1047
- Methylenedianiline - 1910.1050
- 1,3-Butadiene - 1910.1051

What are the minimum elements of an emergency action plan?

- Procedures for reporting fires and other emergencies.
- Procedures for emergency evacuation, including the type of evacuation and *exit route* assignments.
- Procedures for employees who stay behind to continue critical plant operations.
- Procedures to account for all employees after evacuation.
- Procedures for employees performing rescue or medical duties.
- Name or job title of employees to contact for detailed plan information.
- Alarm system to alert workers.

In addition, you must designate and train employees to assist in a safe and orderly evacuation of other employees. You must also review the emergency action plan with each employee covered when the following occur:

- Plan is developed or an employee is assigned initially to a job.
- Employee's responsibilities under the plan changes.
- Plan is changed.

Must all employers have fire prevention plans?

If you have *10 or fewer employees*, you may communicate your plan orally. If you have *more than 10 employees*, however, your plan must be written, kept in the workplace, and available for employee review. Although employers are only required to have a fire prevention plan (FPP) when the applicable OSHA standard requires it, OSHA strongly recommends that all employers have a fire prevention plan (FPP). The following OSHA standards require FPPs:

- Ethylene Oxide, 1910.1047
- Methylenedianiline - 1910.1050
- 1,3-Butadiene - 1910.1051

Here are the minimum provisions of a fire prevention plan:

- List of all major fire hazards, proper handling and storage procedures for hazardous materials, potential ignition sources and their control, and the type of fire protection equipment necessary to control each major hazard.
- Procedures to control accumulations of flammable and combustible waste materials.
- Procedures for regular maintenance of safeguards installed on heat-producing equipment to prevent the accidental ignition of combustible materials.
- Name or job title of employees responsible for maintaining equipment to prevent or control sources of ignition or fires.
- Name or job title of employees responsible for the control of fuel source hazards.

In addition, when you assign employees to a job, you must inform them of any fire hazards they may be exposed to. You must also review with each employee those parts of the fire prevention plan necessary for self-protection.

How can I get more information on safety and health?

For more detail on exit routes and related standards see *Exit Routes, Emergency Action Plans, and Fire Prevention Plans* in *Title 29 of the Code of Federal Regulations* (*CFR*) 1910.33-39; and OSHA Directive CPL 2-1.037, *Compliance Policy for Emergency Action Plans and Fire Prevention Plans*. In addition, employers who comply with the exit route provisions of the National Fire Protection Association's 101-2000, *Life Safety Code*, will be considered in compliance with the OSHA requirements for exit routes.

OSHA has various publications, standards, technical assistance, and compliance tools to help you, and offers extensive assistance through workplace consultation, voluntary protection programs, strategic partnerships, alliances, state plans, grants, training, and education. OSHA's *Safety and Health Program Management Guidelines* (54 *Federal Register* 3904-3916, 1/26/89) detail elements critical to the development of a successful safety and health management system. This and other information are available on OSHA's website.

- For one free copy of OSHA publications, send a self-addressed mailing label to OSHA Publications Office, 200 Constitution Avenue N.W., N-3101, Washington, DC 20210; or send a request to our fax at (202) 693-2498, or call us toll-free at (800) 321-OSHA.
- To order OSHA publications online at **www.osha.gov**, go to **Publications** and follow the instructions for ordering.
- To file a complaint by phone, report an emergency, or get OSHA advice, assistance, or products, contact your nearest OSHA office under the U.S. Department of Labor listing in your phone book, or call toll-free at **(800) 321-OSHA (6742)**. The teletypewriter (TTY) number is (877) 889-5627.
- To file a complaint online or obtain more information on OSHA federal and state programs, visit OSHA's website.

This is one in a series of informational fact sheets highlighting OSHA programs, policies, or standards. It does not impose any new compliance requirements. For a comprehensive list of compliance requirements of OSHA standards or regulations, refer to *Title 29 of the Code of Federal Regulations*. This information will be made available to sensory-impaired individuals upon request. The voice phone is (202) 693-1999. See also OSHA's website at **www.osha.gov**.

OSHA
Occupational Safety and Health Administration
U.S. Department of Labor
2003

OSHA Fact Sheet

Planning and Responding to Workplace Emergencies

Nobody expects an emergency or disaster. Yet emergencies and disasters can strike anyone, anytime, anywhere. Employers should establish effective safety and health management systems and prepare their workers to handle emergencies before they arise.

Planning

Where required by some Occupational Safety and Health Administration standards, firms with more than 10 employees must have a written emergency action plan; smaller companies may communicate their plans orally. Top management support and the commitment and involvement of all employees are essential to an effective emergency action plan.

Employers should review plans with employees when initially put in place and re-evaluate and amend the plan periodically whenever the plan itself, or employee responsibilities, change. Emergency procedures, including the handling of any toxic chemicals, should include:
- Escape procedures and escape route assignments.
- Special procedures for employees who perform or shut down critical plant operations.
- Systems to account for all employees after evacuation and for information about the plan.
- Rescue and medical duties for employees who perform them.
- Means for reporting fires and other emergencies.

Chain of Command

The employer should designate an emergency response coordinator and a backup coordinator. The coordinator may be responsible for plant-wide operations, public information and ensuring that outside aid is called. Having a backup coordinator ensures that a trained person is always available. Employees should know who the designated coordinator is. Duties of the coordinator and employer include:
- Determining what emergencies may occur and seeing that emergency procedures are developed to address each situation.
- Directing all emergency activities including evacuation of personnel.
- Ensuring that outside emergency services are notified when necessary.
- Directing the shutdown of plant operations when necessary.

Emergency Response Teams

Emergency response team members should be thoroughly trained for potential crises and physically capable of carrying out their duties. Team members need to know about toxic hazards in the workplace and be able to judge when to evacuate personnel or when to rely on outside help (e.g., when a fire is too large to handle). One or more teams must be trained in:
- Use of various types of fire extinguishers.
- First aid, including cardiopulmonary resuscitation (CPR) and self-contained breathing apparatus (SCBA).
- Requirements of the OSHA bloodborne pathogens standard.
- Shutdown procedures.
- Chemical spill control procedures.
- Search and emergency rescue procedures.
- Hazardous materials emergency response.

Response Activities

Effective emergency communication is vital. An alternate area for a communications center other than management offices should be established in the plans, and the emergency response coordinator should operate from this center. Management should provide emergency alarms and ensure that employees know how to report emergencies. An updated list of key personnel and off-duty telephone numbers should be maintained.

Accounting for personnel following evacuation is critical. A person in the control center should notify police or emergency response team members of persons believed missing.

Effective security procedures can prevent unauthorized access and protect vital records and equipment. Duplicate records of essential accounting files, legal documents and lists of employee relatives – to be notified in case of emergency – can be kept at off-site locations.

Training

Every employee needs to know details of the emergency action plan, including evacuation plans, alarm systems, reporting procedures for personnel, shutdown procedures, and types of potential emergencies. Any special hazards, such as flammable materials, toxic chemicals, radioactive sources or water-reactive substances, should be discussed with employees. Drills should be held at random intervals, at least annually, and should include outside police and fire authorities.

Training must be conducted at least annually and when employees are hired or when their job changes. Additional training is needed when new equipment, materials or processes are introduced, when the layout or design of the facility changes, when procedures have been updated or revised, or when exercises show that employee performance is inadequate.

Personal Protection

Employees exposed to or near accidental chemical splashes, falling objects, flying particles, unknown atmospheres with inadequate oxygen or toxic gases, fires, live electrical wiring, or similar emergencies need appropriate personal protective equipment.

Medical Assistance

First aid must be available within 3 to 4 minutes of an emergency. Worksites more than 3 to 4 minutes from an infirmary, clinic, or hospital should have at least one person on-site trained in first aid (available all shifts), have medical personnel readily available for advice and consultation, and develop written emergency medical procedures.

It is essential that first aid supplies are available to the trained first aid providers, that emergency phone numbers are placed in conspicuous places near or on telephones, and prearranged ambulance services for any emergency are available. It may help to coordinate an emergency action plan with the outsider responders such as the fire department, hospital emergency room, EMS providers and local HAZMAT teams.

Further Information

More detailed information on workplace emergencies is provided in "How to Plan for Workplace Emergencies and Evacuations" (OSHA 3088) available free on OSHA's website or from OSHA Publications, Room N3101, 200 Constitution Ave., N.W., Washington, D.C. 20210, telephone 1-800-321-OSHA, or local OSHA offices. Further information is also available in OSHA's Evacuation Plans and Procedure eTool and Emergency Preparedness and Response webpage

---

This is one in a series of informational fact sheets highlighting OSHA programs, policies or standards. It does not impose any new compliance requirements. For a comprehensive list of compliance requirements of OSHA standards or regulations, refer to Title 29 of the Code of Federal Regulations. This information will be made available to sensory impaired individuals upon request. The voice phone is (202) 693-1999; teletypewriter (TTY) number: (877) 889-5627.

For more complete information:

OSHA Occupational Safety and Health Administration

U.S. Department of Labor
www.osha.gov
(800) 321-OSHA

4/2004

Exit routes, Emergency Action Plans, Fire Prevention Plans, and fire protection

Knowledge check

1. Which of the following statements is TRUE regarding Emergency Action Plans (EAPs)?
    a) EAPs need to be written down only if requested by employees
    b) EAPs facilitate and organize actions taken during an emergency
    c) EAPs have no effect on the number or severity of injuries during and emergency
    d) EAPs increase confusion due to the number of documents required

2. Fire Prevention Plan (FPP) requirements include all of the following, except ____.
    a) it must be written document that is kept in the workplace
    b) it must be made available to employees for review
    c) the employer must review with each employee the parts of the FPP necessary for self-protection
    d) FPPs can be communicated orally if there are more than 10 employees

3. Which of the following elements are required in order for a fire to occur?
    a) Sufficient oxygen, fuel, ignition source, and chemical reaction
    b) Sufficient fuel, carbon dioxide, heat, and chemical reaction
    c) Combustible materials, spark, heat, and mechanical reaction
    d) Smoke, heat, flames, and light reaction

4. Only those employees who have received training on the use of a fire extinguisher can be authorized to use a fire extinguisher during a workplace fire.
    a) True
    b) False

5. Which of the following statements represents an element of a good emergency evacuation floor plan?

   a) Designates one exit pathway so as not to confuse evacuees

   b) Indicates locations of elevators used to reach emergency exit

   c) Directs exits away from rooms with hazardous materials

   d) Indicates restrooms and windows as potential exits

6. Trash fires involving paper and wood products are ___ fires.

   a) Class A

   b) Class B

   c) Class C

   d) Class D

7. Which fire extinguisher is appropriate for use on a fire involving gasoline in a confined space when no respiratory protection is available?

   a) Water (APW) extinguisher

   b) Carbon dioxide extinguisher

   c) Dry chemical extinguisher

   d) Class K dry-type extinguisher

8. The P.A.S.S. technique for using a fire extinguisher means ___.

   a) Position, aim, sweep, slowly

   b) Pull, aim, squeeze, sweep

   c) Point, away, side-to-side

   d) Pin, approach, start, stop

9. At minimum, how often must maintenance checks be performed on portable fire extinguishers?

    a) Once a month

    b) Once a year

    c) Once every two years

    d) Once every five years

Managing safety and health

HAZARD IDENTIFICATION AND ASSESSMENT

ONE OF THE "root causes" of workplace injuries, illnesses, and incidents is the failure to identify or recognize hazards that are present, or that could have been anticipated. A critical element of any effective safety and health program is a proactive, ongoing process to identify and assess such hazards.

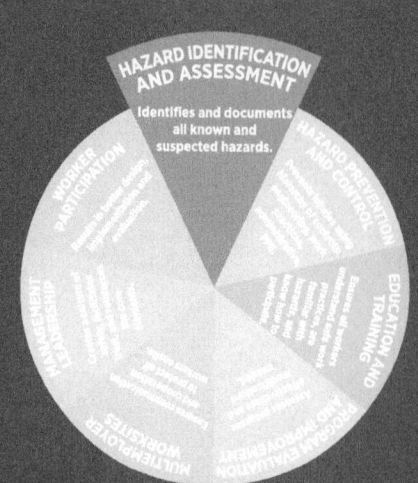

TO IDENTIFY AND ASSESS hazards, employers and workers:

- Collect and review information about the hazards present or likely to be present in the workplace.

- Conduct initial and periodic workplace inspections of the workplace to identify new or recurring hazards.

- Investigate injuries, illnesses, incidents, and close calls/near misses to determine the underlying hazards, their causes, and safety and health program shortcomings.

- Group similar incidents and identify trends in injuries, illnesses, and hazards reported.

- Consider hazards associated with emergency or nonroutine situations.

- For each hazard identified, determine the severity and likelihood of incidents that could result, and use this information to prioritize corrective actions.

Some hazards, such as housekeeping and tripping hazards, can and should be fixed as they are found. Fixing hazards on the spot emphasizes the importance of safety and health and takes advantage of a safety leadership opportunity. Fixing other hazards identified using the processes described here will be addressed in the next section, "Hazard Prevention and Control."

Action item 1: Collect existing information about workplace hazards

Information on workplace hazards may already be available to employers and workers from both internal and external sources.

How to accomplish it

- Collect, organize, and review information with workers to determine what types of hazards may be present and which workers may be exposed or potentially exposed.

- Information available in the workplace may include:
  - Equipment and machinery operating manuals.

- SDSs provided by chemical manufacturers.
- Self-inspection reports and inspection reports from insurance carriers, government agencies, and consultants.
- Records of previous injuries and illnesses, such as OSHA 300 and 301 logs and reports of incident investigations.
- Workers' compensation records and reports.
- Patterns of frequently occurring injuries and illnesses.
- Exposure monitoring results, industrial hygiene assessments, and medical records (appropriately redacted to ensure patient/worker privacy).
- Existing safety and health programs (lockout/tagout, confined spaces, process safety management, PPE, etc.).
- Input from workers, including surveys or minutes from safety and health committee meetings.
- Results of job hazard analyses (JHAs, also known as job safety analyses or JSAs).

• Information about hazards may be available from outside sources, such as:
- OSHA, National Institute for Occupational Safety and Health (NIOSH), and Centers for Disease Control and Prevention (CDC) websites, publications, and alerts.
- Trade associations.
- Labor unions, state and local occupational safety and health committees/coalitions ("COSH groups"), and worker advocacy groups.
- Safety and health consultants.

Action item 2: Inspect the workplace for safety hazards

Hazards can be introduced over time as workstations and processes change, equipment or tools become worn, maintenance is neglected, or housekeeping practices decline. Setting aside time to regularly inspect the workplace for hazards can help identify shortcomings so that they can be addressed before an incident occurs.

How to accomplish it

- Conduct regular inspections of all operations, equipment, work areas, and facilities. Have workers participate on the inspection team, and talk to them about hazards that they see or report.
- Be sure to document inspections so you can later verify that hazardous conditions are corrected. Take photos or video of problem areas to facilitate later discussion and brainstorming about how to control them, and for use as learning aids.
- Include all areas and activities in these inspections, such as storage and warehousing, facility and equipment maintenance, purchasing and office functions, and the activities of on-site contractors, subcontractors, and temporary employees.
- Regularly inspect both plant vehicles (e.g., forklifts, powered industrial trucks) and transportation vehicles (e.g., cars, trucks).
- Use checklists that highlight things to look for. Typical hazards fall into several major categories, such as those listed below; each workplace will have its own list:
  - General housekeeping
  - Slip, trip, and fall hazards

- Electrical hazards
- Equipment operation
- Equipment maintenance
- Fire protection
- Work organization and process flow (including staffing and scheduling)
- Work practices
- Workplace violence
- Ergonomic problems
- Lack of emergency procedures

• Before changing operations, workstations, or workflow; making major organizational changes; or introducing new equipment, materials, or processes, seek the input of workers and evaluate the planned changes for potential hazards and related risks.

Note: Many hazards can be identified using common knowledge and available tools. For example, you can easily identify and correct hazards associated with broken stair rails and frayed electrical cords. Workers can be a very useful internal resource, especially if they are trained in how to identify and assess risks.

Action item 3: Identify health hazards

Identifying workers' exposure to health hazards is typically more complex than identifying physical safety hazards. For example, gases and vapors may be invisible, often have no odor, and may not have an immediately noticeable harmful health effect. Health hazards include chemical hazards (solvents, adhesives, paints, toxic dusts, etc.), physical hazards (noise, radiation, heat, etc.), biological hazards (infectious diseases), and ergonomic risk factors (heavy lifting, repetitive motions, vibration). Reviewing workers' medical records (appropriately redacted to ensure patient/worker privacy) can be useful in identifying health hazards associated with workplace exposures.

How to accomplish it

- Identify *chemical hazards*—review SDSs and product labels to identify chemicals in your workplace that have low exposure limits, are highly volatile, or are used in large quantities or in unventilated spaces. Identify activities that may result in skin exposure to chemicals.

- Identify *physical hazards*—identify any exposures to excessive noise (areas where you must raise your voice to be heard by others), elevated heat (indoor and outdoor), or sources of radiation (radioactive materials, X-rays, or radiofrequency radiation).

- Identify *biological hazards*—determine whether workers may be exposed to sources of infectious diseases, molds, toxic or poisonous plants, or animal materials (fur or scat) capable of causing allergic reactions or occupational asthma.

- Identify *ergonomic risk factors*—examine work activities that require heavy lifting, work above shoulder height, repetitive motions, or tasks with significant vibration.

- Conduct quantitative exposure assessments, when possible, using air sampling or direct reading instruments.

- Review medical records to identify cases of musculoskeletal injuries, skin irritation or dermatitis, hearing loss, or lung disease that may be related to workplace exposures.

Note: Identifying and assessing health hazards may require specialized knowledge. Small businesses can obtain free and confidential occupational safety and health advice services, including help identifying and assessing workplace hazards, through OSHA's On-site Consultation Program (see www.osha.gov/dcsp/smallbusiness/consult.html).

Action item 4: Conduct incident investigations

Workplace incidents—including injuries, illnesses, close calls/near misses, and reports of other concerns—provide a clear indication of where hazards exist. By thoroughly investigating incidents and reports, you will identify hazards that are likely to cause future harm. The purpose of an investigation must always be to identify the root causes (and there is often more than one) of the incident or concern, in order to prevent future occurrences.

How to accomplish it

- Develop a clear plan and procedure for conducting incident investigations, so that an investigation can begin immediately when an incident occurs. The plan should cover items such as:
  - Who will be involved
  - Lines of communication
  - Materials, equipment, and supplies needed
  - Reporting forms and templates
- Train investigative teams on incident investigation techniques, emphasizing objectivity and open-mindedness throughout the investigation process.

- Conduct investigations with a trained team that includes representatives of both management and workers.

- Investigate close calls/near misses.

- Identify and analyze root causes to address underlying program shortcomings that allowed the incidents to happen.

- Communicate the results of the investigation to managers, supervisors, and workers to prevent recurrence.

Note: OSHA has special reporting requirements for work-related incidents that lead to serious injury or a fatality (29 CFR 1904.39). OSHA must be notified within 8 hours of a work-related fatality, and within 24 hours of an amputation, loss of an eye, or inpatient hospitalization.

Note: Effective incident investigations do not stop at identifying a single factor that triggered an incident. They ask the questions "Why?" and "What led to the failure?" For example, if a piece of equipment fails, a good investigation asks: "Why did it fail?" "Was it maintained properly?" "Was it beyond its service life?" and "How could this failure have been prevented?" Similarly, a good incident investigation does not stop when it concludes that a worker made an error. It asks such questions as: "Was the worker provided with appropriate tools and time to do the work?" "Was the worker adequately trained?" and "Was the worker properly supervised?"

Action item 5: Identify hazards associated with emergency and nonroutine situations

Emergencies present hazards that need to be recognized and understood. Nonroutine or infrequent tasks, including maintenance and startup/shutdown activities, also present potential hazards. Plans and procedures need to be developed for responding appropriately and safely to hazards associated with foreseeable emergency scenarios and nonroutine situations.

How to accomplish it

- Identify foreseeable emergency scenarios and nonroutine tasks, taking into account the types of material and equipment in use and the location within the facility. Scenarios such as the following may be foreseeable:
  - Fires and explosions
  - Chemical releases
  - Hazardous material spills
  - Startups after planned or unplanned equipment shutdowns
  - Nonroutine tasks, such as infrequently performed maintenance activities
  - Structural collapse
  - Disease outbreaks
  - Weather emergencies and natural disasters
  - Medical emergencies
  - Workplace violence

Action item 6: Characterize the nature of identified hazards, identify interim control measures, and prioritize the hazards for control

The next step is to assess and understand the hazards identified and the types of incidents that could result from worker exposure to those hazards. This information can be used to develop interim controls and to prioritize hazards for permanent control (see "Hazard Prevention and Control").

How to accomplish it

- Evaluate each hazard by considering the severity of potential outcomes, the likelihood that an event or exposure will occur, and the number of workers who might be exposed.

- Use interim control measures to protect workers until more permanent solutions can be implemented.

- Prioritize the hazards so that those presenting the greatest risk are addressed first. Note, however, that employers have an ongoing obligation to control all serious recognized hazards and to protect workers.

Note: "Risk" is the product of hazard and exposure. Thus, risk can be reduced by controlling or eliminating the hazard, or by reducing workers' exposure to hazards. An assessment of risk helps employers understand hazards in the context of their own workplace, and prioritize hazards for permanent control.

HAZARD PREVENTION AND CONTROL

EFFECTIVE CONTROLS protect workers from workplace hazards; help avoid injuries, illnesses, and incidents; minimize or eliminate safety and health risks; and help employers provide workers with safe and healthful working conditions. The processes described in this section will help employers prevent and control hazards identified in the previous section.

TO EFFECTIVELY CONTROL and prevent hazards, employers should:

- Involve workers, who often have the best understanding of the conditions that create hazards and insights into how they can be controlled.

- Identify and evaluate options for controlling hazards, using a "hierarchy of controls."

- Use a hazard control plan to guide the selection and implementation of controls, and implement controls according to the plan.

- Develop plans with measures to protect workers during emergencies and nonroutine activities.

- Evaluate the effectiveness of existing controls to determine whether they continue to provide protection, or whether different controls may be more effective. Review new technologies for their potential to be more protective, more reliable, or less costly.

Action item 1: Identify control options

A wealth of information exists to help employers investigate options for controlling identified hazards. Before selecting any control options, it is essential to solicit workers' input on their feasibility and effectiveness.

How to accomplish it

- Review sources such as OSHA standards and guidance, industry consensus standards, NIOSH publications, manufacturers' literature, and engineering reports to identify potential control measures. Keep current on relevant information from trade or professional associations.

- Investigate control measures used in other workplaces and determine whether they would be effective at your workplace.

- Get input from workers who may be able to suggest and evaluate solutions based on their knowledge of the facility, equipment, and work processes.

- For complex hazards, consult with safety and health experts, including OSHA's On-site Consultation Program.

Action item 2: Select controls

Employers should select the controls that are the most feasible, effective, and permanent.

How to accomplish it

- Eliminate or control all serious hazards (hazards that are causing or are likely to cause death or serious physical harm) immediately.

- Use interim controls while you develop and implement longer-term solutions.

- Select controls according to a hierarchy that emphasizes engineering solutions (including elimination or substitution) first, followed by safe work practices, administrative controls, and finally PPE.

- Avoid selecting controls that may directly or indirectly introduce new hazards. Examples include exhausting contaminated air into occupied work spaces or using hearing protection that makes it difficult to hear backup alarms.

- Review and discuss control options with workers to ensure that controls are feasible and effective.

- Use a combination of control options when no single method fully protects workers.

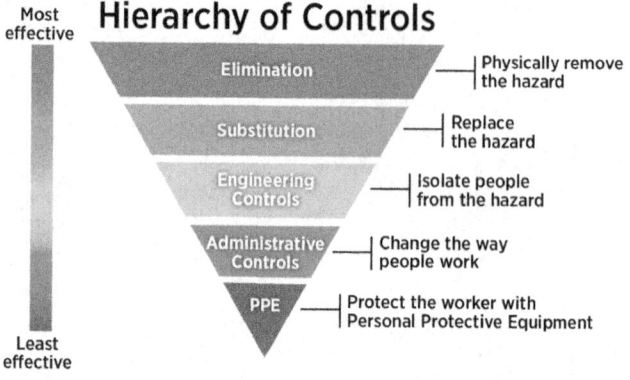

Source: NIOSH

Note: Whenever possible, select equipment, machinery, and materials that are inherently safer based on the application of "Prevention through Design" (PtD) principles. Apply PtD when making your own facility, equipment, or product design decisions. For more information, see the link to the NIOSH PtD initiative on the recommended practices Web page.

Action item 3: Develop and update a hazard control plan

A hazard control plan describes how the selected controls will be implemented. An effective plan will address serious hazards first. Interim controls may be necessary, but the overall goal is to ensure effective long-term control of hazards. It is important to track progress toward completing the control plan, and periodically (at least annually and when conditions, processes, or equipment change) verify that controls remain effective.

How to accomplish it

- List the hazards needing controls in order of priority.

- Assign responsibility for installing or implementing the controls to a specific person or persons with the power or ability to implement the controls.

- Establish a target completion date.
- Plan how you will track progress toward completion.
- Plan how you will verify the effectiveness of controls after they are installed or implemented.

Action item 4: Select controls to protect workers during nonroutine operations and emergencies

The hazard control plan should include provisions to protect workers during nonroutine operations and foreseeable emergencies. Depending on the workplace, these could include fires, explosions, chemical releases, hazardous material spills, unplanned equipment shutdowns, infrequent maintenance activities, natural and weather disasters, workplace violence, terrorist or criminal attacks, disease outbreaks (e.g., pandemic influenza), or medical emergencies. Nonroutine tasks, or tasks workers don't normally do, should be approached with particular caution. Prior to initiating such work, review JSAs/JHAs with any workers involved and notify others about the nature of the work, work schedule, and any necessary precautions.

How to accomplish it

- Develop procedures to control hazards that may arise during nonroutine operations (e.g., removing machine guarding during maintenance and repair).
- Develop or modify plans to control hazards that may arise in emergency situations.
- Procure any equipment needed to control emergency-related hazards.
- Assign responsibilities for implementing the emergency plan.
- Conduct emergency drills to ensure that procedures and equipment provide adequate protection during emergency situations.

Note: Depending on your location, type of business, and materials stored or used on site, authorities including local fire and emergency response departments, state agencies, the U.S. Environmental Protection Agency, the Department of Homeland Security, and OSHA may have additional requirements for emergency plans. Ensure that your procedures comply with these requirements.

Action item 5: Implement selected controls in the workplace

Once hazard prevention and control measures have been identified, they should be implemented according to the hazard control plan.

How to accomplish it

- Implement hazard control measures according to the priorities established in the hazard control plan.
- When resources are limited, implement measures on a "worst-first" basis, according to the hazard ranking priorities (risk) established during hazard identification and assessment. (Note, however, that regardless of limited resources, employers have an obligation to protect workers from recognized, serious hazards.)
- Promptly implement any measures that are easy and inexpensive—such as general housekeeping, removal of obvious tripping hazards such as electrical cords, and basic lighting—regardless of the level of hazard they involve.

Action item 6: Follow up to confirm that controls are effective

To ensure that control measures are and remain effective, employers should track progress in implementing controls, inspect and evaluate controls once they are installed, and follow routine preventive maintenance practices.

How to accomplish it

- Track progress and verify implementation by asking the following questions:
  - Have all control measures been implemented according to the hazard control plan?
  - Have engineering controls been properly installed and tested?
  - Have workers been appropriately trained so that they understand the controls, including how to operate engineering controls, safe work practices, and PPE use requirements?
  - Are controls being used correctly and consistently?

- Conduct regular inspections (and industrial hygiene monitoring, if indicated) to confirm that engineering controls are operating as designed.

- Evaluate control measures to determine if they are effective or need to be modified. Involve workers in the evaluation of the controls. If controls are not effective, identify, select, and implement further control measures that will provide adequate protection.

- Confirm that work practices, administrative controls, and PPE use policies are being followed.

- Conduct routine preventive maintenance of equipment, facilities, and controls to help prevent incidents due to equipment failure.

Books in the OSHA Outreach Training Program Series

General Industry

OSHA 10-Hour General Industry; Student Workbook
(ISBN-13: 978-1979408592)

OSHA 10 horas industria general; cuaderno de trabajo para el estudiante
(ISBN-13: 978-1719168144)

OSHA 30-Hour General Industry; Student Workbook
(ISBN-13: 978-1719167451)

OSHA 30 horas industria general; cuaderno de trabajo para el estudiante
(ISBN-13: 978-1719168328)

Construction

OSHA 10-Hour Construction; Student Workbook
(ISBN-13: 978-1546484363)

OSHA 10 horas construcción; cuaderno de trabajo para el estudiante
(ISBN-13: 978-1974103553)

OSHA 30-Hour Construction; Student Workbook
(ISBN-13: 978-1975997830)

OSHA 30 horas construcción; cuaderno de trabajo para el estudiante
(ISBN-13: 978-1977837479)

OSHA 10 horas construcción; manual para el instructor (coming soon)

Search by author, title or ISBN in your favorite online bookstore

Made in the USA
Columbia, SC
25 March 2024